How to Talk to Anyone

Master Small Talk, Improve Your Social Skills, and Build Meaningful Relationships

Marcus Smith

This book is dedicated to my beloved wife

Table of Contents

Your Free Gift

As a way of saying thank you for purchasing this book, I am offering a book (The Single Biggest Mistake in Communication) for **FREE** to my readers.

To get instant access just go to:

www.lazybonespublishing.com/optin1

Inside the book, you will discover:

- How humans actually communicate with each other
- A breakdown of what the biggest mistake in communication is
- A simple and practical guide to resolve the problem

Make sure to grab your free copy today!

Introduction

Do you have a tough time communicating with others? Do you feel anxious or constantly worried when you have to talk to someone new? Are you in a world of despair because you believe you do not have the required communication skills? Are you unable to build meaningful and healthy relationships due to this? Do you want to improve your communication skills but don't know where to start? If yes, stop worrying because this is the perfect book for you.

Communication is one of the most important aspects of human life. It is the basis of forming and maintaining relationships. A conversation with a stranger can transform into a lasting and healthy relationship when you know how to talk. Don't worry if you're not good at it because there is always room for improvement. If you are struggling with it right now, this doesn't have to be a permanent situation in your life. You have complete control over changing it. Yes, you read that right! You might look at some and wonder how they do it! How can they talk to others without an ounce of worry or anxiety? What if you could do the same? All it requires is a little commitment and effort on your part.

In this book, you will learn about everything associated with communicating with others. This book will act as your detailed step-by-step guide and help overcome challenges you are facing while communicating with others. It will also show you how to build meaningful and healthy relationships. The first thing you need to do is change your mindset to a positive one. Negative thoughts are detrimental to change and improvement because they hold you back. By identifying and overcoming negative thoughts associated with social interactions, it becomes easier to improve your communication skills. Unknowingly we also develop a variety of bad habits that hamper our social interactions. Whether it is the urge to constantly correct, get distracted, or talk over others, these habits need to be avoided. The good news is that identifying these bad habits is incredibly easy. With a little conscious effort and patience you can break these habits and develop healthier ones. This, in turn, will improve the quality of your social interactions.

Communication is not just restricted to the words you utter. It also includes your body language. Understanding the importance of body language and improving it will make it easier to approach a stranger and strike up a conversation. You will also be provided a variety of tips and options that can be used for initiating a conversation with anyone. If you usually struggle to strike up a conversation or make small talk, you can fix this situation within no time. Apart from all this, you will also be introduced to the importance of becoming an active listener. Becoming an active listener offers a variety of benefits and the most important one is that it paves the way for meaningful conversations and relationships.

An effective relationship cannot be established if you cannot communicate. Open and honest communication is the basis for a healthy relationship. The simple steps you can follow to transition from a conversation with a stranger to creating a meaningful relationship are included in this book. This will help you develop and maintain meaningful and lasting relationships. Apart from all this, you will also be given some practical suggestions for maintaining a positive dialogue. This will further enhance the quality of relationships you have in life. It also enables you to stay away from toxic relationships. A combination of all these factors will significantly improve the quality of your life.

Are you wondering how I know this? Well, I believe it is time for an introduction. Hello, my name is Marcus Smith. Regardless of whether you want to become better at communicating with others or overcome the anxiety and fear you experience when you have to talk to others, it can be solved. The wonderful thing about life is that it is never too late to change. Once you put your mind to it, you can overcome anything, and I truly believe this. For over five years, I've been studying and researching communication and the different aspects involved in it. I not only understand the workings of communication but have used all the information I collected to improve my own life. This is one topic I'm incredibly passionate about. I think the process starts with arming yourself with the right information. This is where I will help you. I will act as your guide every step of the way and help improve your communication skills. Don't feel overwhelmed or worry that you are the only one who cannot talk to others. There are several like you out there.

Over the years, I started learning, researching, and studying communication. The information and tips provided, along with my personal experience, will help you become better at communicating. I know you can do it because even I did. It is not a complicated or an anxiety-inducing process. Instead, it's about making small changes every day to achieve the goal you desire. Once you master the art of communication, the quality of your life and relationships will improve in ways you never expected. All this will leave you feeling pleasantly surprised.

So, are you eager to learn more about all this? Do you want to improve your communication skills? Do you want to discover the secrets to striking a conversation with anyone? If yes, what are you waiting for? There is no time like the present to get started! Remember you are not alone and

I'm going to walk you through the process until you've mastered everything required to be able to talk to anyone. Are you ready to meet and talk with new people? If yes, keep reading!

Chapter 1
Conquer Your Negative Thoughts

Before I start teaching you the relevant tools that will help improve your communication skills, we need to talk about the elephant in the room, and that is negativity. There isn't one specific reason that causes negative thinking. Instead, it's a variety of factors both internal and external that regulate our thoughts. Let's dive deeper into this topic.

When it comes to life, your mindset plays a crucial role. Your mindset is regulated by your thoughts. Your thoughts are incredibly powerful because they have the power to influence your behaviors. If you are struggling with negative thoughts then understanding where they come from, the consequences associated with them, and how to overcome them is needed.

If you constantly worry about social interactions in a negative context, it will not amount to anything good. These negative thoughts can trigger a variety of unpleasant emotions, such as: anxiety, frustration, fear, or even anger. If all this is left unchecked, it ultimately results in the creation of a warped persona that not only impacts how you present yourself, but all your relationships too. Social interactions at this stage will become extremely difficult. It might feel as if any conversation is doomed to fail before it even starts. However, you don't have to worry because the good news is that you have the power to ensure this doesn't happen. The first step toward self-improvement is to learn to tackle your negative thoughts.

What Causes Negative Thoughts?

The brain is the most powerful yet complicated organ in the body. It is responsible for all our functions. Whatever we feel, think, or experience is determined by this organ that is securely sitting within the skull. A popular notion about negativity is that it is a small part of our adaptive evolutionary function. It essentially means negativity, to a certain degree, helped our ancestors survive. Therefore, it was passed over to future generations through the genes. For instance, the fight or flight response is responsible for our survival. This instinct is also embedded in our genes. Negative events such as dealing with predators or starvation were nothing less than matters of life and death for our ancestors. Their focus on such negative events is what makes them more sensitive to any stimuli associated with these events and improves their chances of survival. Unfortunately, this also means that these negative traits have been passed on to generations to come.

It is interesting to know that, at times, it is easier to be negative than to be positive. This is because our brain knows how to prioritize information. Due to our genetic coding, the brain prioritizes negative information over positive information. This is because it believes such information could be related to a threat. From a young age, this enables us to learn about different circumstances we should avoid so we do not end up getting hurt. This adaptation has kept our species alive but unfortunately, it has also increased negative thinking.

In this section, let's look at different factors that are responsible for negative thoughts.

Negativity Bias

As mentioned earlier, it is easier to think negative thoughts than positive ones. Negativity bias essentially refers to how the impact of negative events is much greater on individuals than that of positive ones. It's a general inclination to utilize negative information more than positive information. If all this sounds extremely complicated, then simply think about the time you spend ruminating about mistakes made in the past or worrying about the future. Even though you have no control over these situations and you know these thoughts are not going to amount to anything, can you stop? If not, it is a negativity bias. It also displays how we are affected by negative events more than positive ones. A simple example of this is we are more sensitive to any criticism we receive than praise.

Maintaining Negativity

Any event in the past that set you on a path toward negativity is called the initial cause. This is usually a traumatic experience that scars us in some way. For instance, a child who was bullied can carry the notion that they are unlovable or incapable of striking friendships. However, there is something also called the maintaining cause. This is when our different habits unintentionally end up feeding our negative mindset.

These unhealthy habits ensure that negativity doesn't go away and instead grows even stronger. For instance, some people have a negative association with talking on the phone, and when receiving a phone call, they simply avoid it. This teaches the brain that answering phone calls is dangerous and it must be avoided. This means that the next time the person faces a phone call, they will likely feel even more anxious than the last time. This creates a cycle where the person is avoiding the situation, but by doing so they are reinforcing the negative message to their brain. This shows how negative thinking doesn't necessarily have to come from one specific situation from the past.

Negative Self-Talk

Negative self-talk essentially refers to how negativity can seep into self-talk. Self-talk, as the name suggests, refers to the internal conversations or dialogue you have with yourself. For instance, "I will never be good at this and I should not even try because what is the point if I'll never be good?" is an example of negative self-talk. The musings of your inner critic are what negative self-talk looks like. The problem with negative self-talk is this undesirable inner dialogue ultimately affects how you think and feel not just about yourself but the world in general. It results in a variety of other problems such as limited thinking, desire for perfectionism, increases feelings of depression, and can cause relationship challenges.

Role of the Subconscious Mind

As mentioned previously, the brain has a lot of power and it is responsible for all the thoughts you think. It keeps forming new neurological connections and patterns. These connections may be desirable or potentially unhelpful. They are determined by all that you have endured. These patterns were not developed overnight. Instead, they are developed by the thought patterns that are stuck in your subconscious. However, the subconscious is not always your friend and can become your biggest enemy.

The subconscious mind is programmed to keep us away from pain and increase the happiness or pleasure we experience. This is a basic human instinct. For instance, would you touch a hot pan? You wouldn't and this is an involuntary action that tells your brain touching the hot pan is going to cause pain. Similarly, the brain also shies away from thoughts, events, or situations that trigger similar pain. The longer you keep thinking or doing things that reinforce the negative thought you have, the stronger it becomes. The only way to break free of this pattern is to consciously focus on shifting your internal dialogue and reprogramming the subconscious.

Consequences of a Negative Mindset

The mindset you maintain matters because it ultimately influences not just how you feel but what you think as well. It is directly responsible for your behavior, which in turn is responsible for shaping your life. When you are happy, chances are you have better control over stress, and have a positive outlook toward life in general. On the other hand, it may feel like you are going through life with a personal rain cloud over your head when you have a negative mindset. Learning about the consequences of a negative mindset makes it easier to see why you need to change it.

Reduces the Ability to Achieve Goals

Your ability to achieve the goals you have set for yourself is affected by a negative mindset. When your inner critic is constantly telling you that you cannot do something or are not good enough, it increases self-doubt. It also increases self-sabotaging behaviors, which ultimately get in the way of achieving your goals. If you don't believe in yourself, how can you find the motivation needed to achieve your desires?

Increases Stress

A negative mindset increases the stress you are experiencing. Understand that we already lead extremely hectic and stressful lives these days. Any source of added stress is unwelcome. If your mindset itself becomes a source of stress, life can become unbearable. A negative mindset zeroes in on all the things you think are missing from your life. If you are only fixated on the negative aspects, any trace of joy or happiness is eliminated from your life. This, in turn, will increase the stress you are experiencing.

Reduces Self-Esteem and Confidence

A combination of all the factors mentioned until now gets in the way of healthy self-esteem and confidence. When you feel poorly about yourself or constantly put yourself down, it harms your self-esteem. This hampers your ability to believe in yourself and your skills, which further reduces self-confidence. It, in turn, increases stress, promotes a negative mindset, and harms different aspects of your life. A negative mindset creates a vicious cycle of negativity that trickles into every aspect of your life and every role you play.

Relationship Challenges

A negative mindset gets in the way of developing and maintaining healthy relationships. For instance, a simple disagreement with your partner might immediately take your thoughts to the worst case scenario. Amplifying the problem more than it should, which might make you think the worst of them or even yourself. It forces you to start second-guessing everything. It increases self-doubt, reduces self-confidence, and prevents you from seeing the good. When all these things are put together, it automatically creates more problems in any relationship.

Overcoming a Negative Mindset

Now that you are aware of all the different problems associated with a negative mindset, it is time to break free of it. The good news is you have complete control over your thoughts. Your mind is within your control, and you can dictate what you are supposed to think. You are not helpless and it is time to regain control over your mindset and change it for the better.

The simplest way to minimize negativity in your life is by becoming aware of your thoughts. Self-awareness is needed to understand your emotional experiences. When you are aware of your emotional state then you are in control of it. Instead of letting it control you, you can regulate it. After all, how can you solve a problem if you don't even know it exists? For instance, self-awareness enables you to understand not just the emotions you're experiencing, but their causes and how they make you feel. These factors automatically give you better control over your thoughts.

Overcome Negativity Bias

To overcome negativity bias, focus on the good in your life. It is about concentrating on gratitude instead of worrying about all that's missing. It's about looking for the silver lining. There will be numerous instances when even the best-laid plans falter. In such situations, you can either be morose about it or look for the silver lining. Regardless of how a situation seems, there is always something to be learned or understood from it. Doing this will automatically shift your perspective. Instead of focusing on all that's wrong, you can train your mind to look for the good.

Reduce Negative Self-Talk

We all have an inner critic that refuses to stop. It's okay to indulge in negative self-talk from time to time. However, if this becomes a habit, it creates a negative mindset. Negative self-talk results in limited thinking, feelings of depression, challenges relationships, and increases the need for perfectionism. A combination of these factors automatically reduces your overall sense of happiness and increases stress. However, no need to worry because you can reduce negative self-talk by doing the following.

The first thing you need to do is catch your inner critic. Notice when you are being extremely critical of yourself. Stop whenever you say things to yourself that you wouldn't say to a friend or a loved one. Understand that your thoughts and feelings are not always absolute. Negative thoughts about yourself are a skewed perspective of what has or might happen. Learn to contain your negativity and the damage caused by the inner voice. Indulge your inner critic for 10-15 minutes daily. It probably sounds counterintuitive, but it works. Whenever you catch yourself thinking negative thoughts during the day, remind yourself that you will get time to do it later.

As mentioned, your thoughts and feelings are not always synonymous with reality. So, you have the power to change the negativity to something better. You should also focus on cross-examining your inner critic. For instance, if your inner critic says, "I cannot do this," "I will never be good enough," change it to something more neutral. Instead of telling yourself that you cannot do something, changing it to, "This is rather challenging," or "It will require more effort than I previously thought," does the trick.

Further, instead of accepting everything your inner critic says, start to question it. If your inner critic says you are not good enough, ask yourself why you believe it. When you do this, you will realize that most of the things going on in your head are a vast exaggeration and calling yourself out on them reduces the damage it causes. Start focusing on talking to yourself the way you would talk to a friend or a child. Would you be harsh to a loved one? Would you be mean to them or would you call them names? If you wouldn't be mean to them, then what makes you think it is okay to be harsh on yourself? Ensure that you are being kind to yourself. By making your inner voice more compassionate, it will become easier to overcome negative thinking.

Track Your Mood

Tracking your mood is an effective means to regulate it. Whether it is work-related stress or problems arising in a personal relationship, it affects your mood. Using a mood tracker helps identify the causes of certain reactions. How different factors affect mood, and what you can do to gain control over the situation can also be understood. These days, a variety of apps are also available online that can be used for tracking your mood. Apart from that, you can also maintain a journal to get a better understanding of your mood. Start by naming the emotion you're experiencing, identify its causes, and make a note of the behaviors it prompts. After this, try to ask yourself whether the emotions you are experiencing are appropriate for the situation. If not, consider the steps you can take to tolerate the situation. When you learn to track your mood, it makes you more aware of your feelings, the reasons for them, and your responses to them. This goes a long way in limiting a negative mindset.

Start Journaling

Journaling is a wonderful means to gain better control over your thoughts. Every day, spend at least 5-10 minutes making a note of anything good that has happened to you. It doesn't matter whether it is big or small. It can be something as simple as a wonderful meal you had for lunch. When you focus on all the good in your life, it becomes easier to change your mindset. Doing this regularly makes it easier to focus on the good and not just everything that's missing.

Use Positive Affirmations

Affirmations are positive statements that help train your conscious and subconscious mind to let go of negative thinking patterns. Whenever a statement is spoken with conviction, it has the power to alter how you think, feel, behave, and believe. When these statements are used consciously, it helps put a positive spin on your mindset. Positive affirmations can be created and used in any aspect of your life. It's simply about training your mind to look at the good instead of worrying about all that is missing. It helps change negative thought patterns and influences the subconscious to develop more positive beliefs.

For instance, if you think that you are not good enough, you can replace it with a positive affirmation such as, "I am sufficient the way I am." you can write the affirmations down in a journal, and repeat them out loud, or even repeat them mentally. The more you practice positive affirmations, the stronger they become and the easier it is to believe them.

Summary

Let's quickly summarize the key points that were discussed in this chapter:

- The first step in improving your communication skills is to overcome any mental hurdles; in this case, we want to correct having a negative mindset.

- A negative mindset will prevent you from reaching your goals, limit the growth of your relationships, and reduce your overall happiness.

- There are key factors that explain why people can have a negative mindset, they are the following: being biased towards your negative thoughts, maintaining bad habits that generate negativity, negative self-talk, and the chase for pleasure over pain.

- To overcome a negative mindset you need to become aware of these negative thoughts as they occur and to address them.

Call to Action

At the end of applicable chapters, there will be a call to action. The purpose of a call to action is to provide you a tangible takeaway that you can use to help resolve the issue. For this chapter, let's have a look at the call to action that will help fix a negative mindset.

Mood Tracker

- Go to your personal device, access the app store, and find a mood tracker app that works for you.

Alternatively, you can set-up a manual journal on either your personal device or on a written notepad.

- The next time you feel a negative emotion capture it in either the app of your choice or in your journal. Make sure to reflect on these emotions each time and determine why they occurred.

Journaling

- Go to your personal device, access the app store, and find a journal app that works for you. Alternatively, you can set-up a manual journal on either your personal device or on a written notepad.

- When first starting this process, I recommend setting a reminder in your personal device to ensure that you are setting aside time to complete the task.

- Every morning, spend 5-10 minutes writing a few feel good moments from the previous day. If you cannot think of anything from the previous day then reflect back on the week. This will help set the tone for the day.

Affirmations

- Set a time, at least twice a day, to spend a few minutes repeating positive affirmations that relate to you. At the start, I would recommend doing this when you wake up and just before bed.

- When first starting this process, I recommend setting a reminder in your personal device to ensure that you are setting aside time to complete the task.
- To find relatable affirmations, I recommend exploring examples online. Simply, type the following in a search engine (e.g. google), "affirmation examples". This will provide several websites/resources that help you narrow down the affirmations that are most applicable and beneficial for your mindset.

Rewards

- Whenever you successfully journal, track a mood, or do your affirmations for the day, make sure to give yourself a reward. This reward will reinforce the behavior or habit that you are trying to add in your life. Just make sure the reward is healthy for both the mind and body. In my case, I simply use a habit/productivity tracker on my phone. Each time I complete a task for the day, I simply check it off the list. I get a small dopamine rush and I feel better for doing so. Find what works best for you!

Chapter 2
Breaking Your Bad Habits

There is a famous quote by Aristotle that goes along the lines of, "we are what we repeatedly do." This is especially true when it comes to the formation and maintenance of habits. Habits are not formed overnight. When certain behavioral patterns are repeated, they become etched into our neural pathways. For instance, how many times do you use your smartphone to read text messages, scroll through social media, or update any of your online profiles? Do you do this because of an active thought such as, "It's time to check my Facebook profile," or does it happen without any specific or conscious thought? It is quite likely that you didn't do it after consciously thinking about it but because you felt like it. This is an example of a habit.

Habits can be both good and bad. Some help us move forward while others hold us back. Habits can be developed in any aspect of your life and communication is not an exception. From interrupting others while they speak to not maintaining eye contact, these are some common bad habits that become a part of our daily conversations. They have a significant effect on our ability to communicate.

Unfortunately, most don't even realize that they have developed poor communication habits. The good news is that you have complete control over your habits. You can break free of undesirable ones and replace them with positive habits. To do this, you must first understand how habits work. In this chapter, you will learn how habits work, how to avoid common bad habits while conversing, and how to fix them to have better conversations.

How Are Habits Formed?

Is there something that took you a long time to learn? Perhaps it took you a while to learn how to parallel park. It might have been difficult initially and that certainly would have required conscious mental effort. But with practice it would have become easier, you could say it became habitual. Parallel parking, exercising, or brushing your teeth are some examples of activities that follow a similar behavioral neurological pattern.

Habits are classified as passive and active. Passive habits occur when you are repeatedly exposed to certain environments and your body gets used to them. For instance, the bodies of high-altitude climbers gradually adapt to lower levels of oxygen. On the other hand, some habits are known as active habits because they are developed through repeated effort and intention. These are habits that we can perform with little or any conscious thought. Some common activities that belong to this category include brushing our teeth or even tying our shoes. If you are tying your shoes for the first time it requires conscious effort. As you keep practicing, it automatically becomes a habit and comes automatically.

Every habit always begins with a psychological pattern known as the habit loop. It is a three-part process. The first aspect is a cue or a trigger. The second step is the routine and the final step is the reward. The cue or the trigger essentially directs the brain to shift to an automatic mode, which leads to the behavior that unfolds. The routine is the behavior itself. It refers to everything that we commonly think about upon hearing the word habit. The final step is the reward. It is the result that the brain likes, and it helps remember the above-mentioned habit loop.

The habit-making behaviors are associated with a part of the brain known as the basal ganglia. It plays a crucial role in the development of emotions, formation and storage of memories, and recognition of patterns. Another part of the brain known as the prefrontal cortex is responsible for decision-making functions. Once a behavior or routine becomes automatic, the decision-making part of the brain is no longer at play and is instead functioning in a sleep mode like state. In this stage, the brain can completely shut itself down but still perform the same action with minimal mental activity and effort. That's why it becomes easier to focus on something else while doing activities you are habituated to. Whether it is brushing or even driving, once you get into the groove and do it regularly, you can perform these activities without any conscious effort. You can be thinking and doing something else while performing the above-mentioned. All this is associated with the basal ganglia's ability to turn a behavior into an automatic response.

Conversation Mistakes to Avoid

Making mistakes is incredibly common. You might have heard saying that to err is human. The saying couldn't be truer. This also applies when we make mistakes while conversing. Trying to steer clear of as many bad habits as you possibly can is always good. However, don't stress yourself out to be flawless or perfect when you're conversing with others. Remember you can improve any skill or ability you possess with conscious effort, practice and consistency. This is all that matters. Even if you are not good at it right now, you can always get better.

In this section, you will be introduced to some common bad habits that hinder conversations. By avoiding these bad habits, it will become easier to talk to others. You don't have to worry if you make any or all of these mistakes. Habits can always be changed. Now, it is time to identify any mistakes or bad habits you have unknowingly developed. Once you are aware of them, you can learn to overcome them as well.

Looking at Your Phone

Most of us are constantly looking at our phone, tablet, smartwatch, or any other screen. The problem is, in this high-tech world, we are all glued to different screens. Due to this, we seldom pay attention to others around us or even the happenings. One bad habit that you must overcome to become a good conversationalist is to ensure that you are 100% present in the situation. How would you feel if you are talking to someone, but they are not even looking up from their phone? Or, maybe they are mindlessly scrolling through their social media profiles instead of even glancing at you even once? It wouldn't make you feel good. Well, others will have the same response.

So, if someone is talking to you or you want to talk to someone, ensure that you do not constantly check your phone. Instead, pay attention to the speaker. Be a good listener and be 100% present. When you show someone that you are present, it automatically conveys the message that you are interested in what they are saying. This, in turn, makes it easier to keep the conversation going.

Interrupting

How do you feel when you are speaking and others don't seem to be listening? Perhaps you are sharing a story about something exciting and someone else cuts you off before you could complete it? Or maybe you were eagerly sharing something and someone else finished your sentence for you and then launched into what they had to say? How will you feel in any of these situations? Chances are you will feel frustrated and also annoyed that you are not allowed to complete what you had to say.

Well, you should remember the same thing when you are conversing with others as well. It can be incredibly frustrating for someone when they're constantly interrupted or not allowed to finish their story. Such behavior usually sends the message that you are not interested in what the other person has to say, and that you do not care about it. Regardless of what it is, ensure that you avoid doing this. If you notice that you accidentally interrupted someone else, simply apologize, and ask them to continue. Something as simple as, "I'm so sorry that I cut you off, what were you saying? Or "I'm so sorry that I cut you off. Please finish the story!" Does the trick.

Do Not Monopolize

Ensure that you do not become a monopolizer. Were there instances when it felt like there was only one person who was doing all the talking, even though you were in a group? The problem with monopolizers is they end up taking up more than their fair share of time. Regardless of whether it is a one-on-one interaction or a group conversation, avoid turning into a monopolizer. They are adept at turning any conversation about themselves or making it about what they want to say. However, there can be instances when someone might have unknowingly monopolized the conversation because they are outgoing or talkative. Or, perhaps they were excited and enthusiastic about what they wanted to share. In either case, ensure that you don't do this.

Bragging

Some indulge in blatant and gaudy bragging while others might favor the notion of forcing their selling points into conversations. Listening to someone brag constantly or incessantly is certainly no fun. If you want to impress others or want to make others appreciate you, then you will need to let your achievements come up naturally in the conversation. Do not force it into the topic and do not rush others into it.

You should also be aware of any apparent disparities between those you are talking to. For instance, you might excel in a specific area while the other person you are talking to is sensitive about it. From your perspective, it might sound like an honest and straightforward conversation. However, from the listener's perspective, it probably sounds like bragging.

Also, trying to one-up the other person is equally undesirable. Let's assume that you tell someone you had a fun zip lining experience over the weekend. The other person says you wouldn't know what fun truly is until you tried some other activity. This is a classic example of one-upping others. It not only sounds like you are bragging but is a conversation killer too! Never make the mistake of believing that you should always have the best story or a better experience than others while conversing. In a social setting, remember that you don't have to be the first one to reach the finishing line. If someone is looking for your approval, admiration, or seems proud of something, go ahead and participate in their joy. Don't try to steal the spotlight.

Not Moving From Unproductive Topics

Were there ever conversations where you were trying to ask someone about a topic but they seemed uninterested or unenthusiastic about it and are giving you brief responses?

If this happens, ensure that you change the topic and move on to something else. Planning to move away from unproductive topics is needed to maintain a conversation. If the other person doesn't seem interested in participating in the conversation, understand that the current topic is not working. There will also be topics where the conversation thread does not move anywhere. A common reason why most make this mistake is that they are trying to have or keep the interaction interesting. It could also be because they probably have a planned script in their mind and are trying to stick to it. Unfortunately, you cannot dictate conversations and you cannot chalk out what others might want to say or talk about. That said, you could certainly use a list of topics for reference if you want to discuss something. Ensure that you do not force a conversation.

Along the same lines, it's also important to remember that you should not be bringing up any inappropriate topics. Unless you know that whoever you are talking to wouldn't mind, stay away from topics that are offensive, overly personal, or even controversial. It doesn't matter whether you are joking or having a serious discussion. A common reason why most fail to understand this or make this mistake is that they forget the entire world isn't on the same wavelength as them. For instance, some of your family members or even a group of friends might be comfortable dealing with one topic while the others aren't.

Not Listening Well

Listening has become a lost art these days. If you are unwilling to listen, then conversations will just be people trying to talk over each other. Have you ever tried to share or talk about something, but it felt like no one was listening to you? Did you feel discouraged? Did such behavior make you believe that what you were sharing was not worth others' time or attention? How did you feel? Chances are you felt bad, misunderstood, and even disrespected. Well, you shouldn't do this to others. It is incredibly important that you listen when someone else is sharing. If your mind is elsewhere, you are uninterested in the conversation, or your body language conveys the same, chances are others will stop talking to you.

If you are a poor listener, the chances of interrupting others and making other conversational mistakes discussed in this section also increase. When you don't listen, you will not be aware of what others are saying. This means you will end up missing information that was provided to you during the conversation. Poor listening skills or the inability to listen to others can also make you seem self-absorbed. All such depictions automatically kill the conversation. It will reduce the willingness that others have to even talk to you.

Constantly Correcting Others

No two humans are alike and therefore, we have several differences. We are also different in our means or style of communication. A common conversation mistake you must avoid is constantly or pointlessly correcting others. It is rather annoying when someone tries correcting you, especially over minor details. If these details are irrelevant to the overall point they are conveying, then it further worsens the situation. It not only derails the entire flow of the conversation but can make others feel inferior too. Remember, when you correct someone over something pointless, you are calling out their mistake and shining the spotlight on them for the wrong reasons. Depending on the tone used, it can make you seem pedantic, snobby, or even condescending. Since these are all undesirable traits to be associated with, become conscious of how you are talking to others. Some value logic, accuracy, and more over others. If you feel this applies to you, chances are you feel irked when someone says something incorrect. Have you ever felt the need to correct others and feel like the thought is eating you up on the inside when you don't? Well, it is time to change all this!

Before you give in to this urge to correct others, ask yourself what you will gain by doing this. Ask yourself if you are doing more harm than good? Also, consider whether the information you are sharing is something that others want to listen to or even know about. Do you think what others are saying is incorrect or offensive to your values and beliefs? By carefully thinking through these questions, you can reduce the urge to correct others.

Overcome Bad Habits

Every thought, action, or feeling you experience changes the brain in small ways. As mentioned, when an activity is repeated frequently, it becomes a habit. Some are good while others aren't. Regardless of what it is, changing habits is not easy but it is achievable with conscious effort. Now that you are aware of the habit loop, it is time to understand how to change certain habits. Here is a simple example for you to consider.

For instance, Adam goes to Starbucks to spend time with his friends instead of studying at the library. He knows he needs to spend a couple of hours daily studying to maintain his grades. However, spending time with his friends and socializing is what makes him happy. The goal in this scenario is to help implement a routine that enables him to study more and provides the same happy feeling of spending time with his friends. What can he do? One option is that he studies by himself for a while and sees socializing time as a reward for studying. Another option is that he can meet his friends in the library to study and then treat himself at Starbucks.

In both scenarios, Adam is effectively trying to change the routine and reward aspects of the habit loop. It is about disrupting the cue, routine, and reward cycle associated with going to Starbucks or spending time with his friends. Let's look at the habit cycle from a different perspective. For instance, if you are trying to break free of the habit of constantly correcting others in conversations. The cue in the situation is that someone else is talking and you notice they have said something incorrect. The routine is correcting the said person. The reward is feeling better now that you have corrected the other person. Now, it is time to break free of this habit.

The first step is to disrupt the cue. So, whenever someone says something incorrect or makes a mistake you have an option of either correcting them or letting it go. To overcome the habit of correcting others, the first thing you need to do is focus on your conscious thoughts. You will have to consciously stop yourself from correcting others because you will not gain anything from it. Once you have disrupted the cue, you can develop another routine of becoming an active listener. Instead of correcting them, simply listen to what they have to say. Ultimately, the reward is you'll have more pleasant conversations with others and it will help you network and socialize too.

To break free of a habit, you'll have to diagnose its cue, routine, and reward. This gives you better insight into your habits and makes it easier to change them. However, it is important to understand that all habits have a formula or a pattern that your mind follows automatically. To create a new habit loop, you'll have to re-engineer the existing formula. You cannot abruptly end a habit. Instead, you'll have to create a replacement for it. Start by identifying the habit you want to change. After this, identify the cue that triggers it, the routine you follow, and the reward you attain.

Pitfalls to Avoid

When it comes to changing a habit, conscious effort and consistency are needed. Repetition is an important factor when it comes to making a new habit stick. To maintain healthy habits, you must anticipate any hurdles you might run into. Here are some common mistakes most make while working on developing healthy behavior patterns.

Doing Everything at Once

To create a new habit, you will have to make a list of things you are hoping to change or learn. During the initial days, you might have the willpower to succeed. After a while, all the responsibilities of life start piling up, or the urge to indulge in the old habits is triggered. Before you know it, the feeling of being overwhelmed enables you to slowly go back to the previous behavioral patterns. For instance, you might want to exercise regularly. You decide to exercise for an hour at 5 a.m. every day. You stick to the schedule for a couple of days and then give up because it doesn't let you catch up on the rest needed. Or perhaps, the schedule has become too hectic and you cannot follow it. While changing a habit, you must also focus on making the change sustainable. You can do this by picking one thing and doing it well.

Looking for a Big Start

Starting a new habit is not easy. Whenever you are trying to achieve something right away by using maximum effort, it merely increases the difficulty of the task. By doing this, you are essentially setting yourself up for failure. Let us consider that you are developing a habit of exercising regularly. Initially, you might be able to work out for an hour or two daily. After a week, you discover that you cannot devote this significant portion of your time to your exercise regimen. Ultimately you give up on exercising altogether. Most people end up in such situations at one point or another.

When it comes to developing a habit, focus on starting small and easy. It's more about getting used to the routine and doing it instead of focusing on the time spent doing it. If you want to start exercising regularly, the first step is to understand that you just need to start exercising. It doesn't matter whether it is 10 minutes or an hour. Ensure that you are exercising every day without fail. 10 minutes probably doesn't sound like much and doing it for 10 minutes doesn't sound too challenging to maintain. This is exactly what you need to do. Instead of looking for a big start, start small. When the change you need to make looks easy the chances of saying no to it also reduce automatically. This, in turn, makes it easier to ensure the habit sticks.

Pay Attention to the Environment

The environment also matters when it comes to changing a habit and making it stick. Habits are a part of your physical as well as social environment. For instance, the smell of food is a cue that you need to sit and eat. Similarly, seeing the television upon arriving home from work can be a cue to unwind. You can use the environment to ensure the habit sticks. For instance, filling a wall with motivational posters or even sticky notes with inspirational quotes can be beneficial. Talking to your friends, family members, and colleagues about your goals acts as a reminder to stay on track.

Summary

Let's quickly summarize the key points that were discussed in this chapter:

- In order to improve your communication skills, you will need to address any bad habits that you may have created.

- Habits are etched into our brain due to the repetition of a task; once etched into our brain, the habit process can be completed without having to think about it.

- The habit loop consists of three stages: (1) the trigger, (2) the behavior taking place, and (3) the reward.

- There are several common bad habits that can take place during a conversation; these bad habits (e.g. looking at your phone, interrupting others, etc.) will limit your ability to connect with others.

- To overcome a bad habit, you first need to become self-aware of what patterns you are exhibiting; once you have identified a habit that you want to correct, you need to disrupt the habit loop, and replace it with a new one.

Call to Action

Let's have a look at the call to action that will help fix bad habits.

Track Your Bad Habits

- Go to your personal device, access the app store, and find a habit tracker app that works for you. Alternatively, you can set-up a manual journal on either your personal device or on a written notepad.

- The next time you exhibit a behavior that you dislike, capture it in either the app of your choice or in your journal. Make sure to include details from the habit loop: the trigger, the behavior, and the reward. Continue to log these details each time it happens. Eventually, you will notice a pattern will emerge. At this point, you have identified a bad habit.

Replace Bad Habits & Continue to Track

- Once you have identified a bad habit, you will need to disrupt it. Write down what the replacement behavior will be, and how you plan to reward yourself for the new behavior. Each time the trigger occurs, apply the new behavior and the new reward. Remember, without a reward, it will be harder for a new habit to stick.

- Keep track of both the old and new behavior. If you are consistent and patient enough. You will eventually see a reduction in the old behavior and an increase in the new behavior.

Chapter 3
It Starts With Body Language

What is the first thing that pops into your head when you hear the word communication? Chances are you think it is a verbal conversation between two people or more. However, there is so much more to it than just this. Communication also includes the use of body language. The use of non-verbal communication cues can speak louder than any words you say. Your gestures, facial expressions, and eye contact convey a story by themselves. Understanding body language and how to interpret it offers significant insight into becoming an effective communicator. You might have heard that first impressions matter. Did you know that we end up judging people within a second? Well, we do and research suggests the same (Nalini Ambady and Robert Rosenthal, 1993).

So, what is body language? Have you ever looked at a stranger or a friend and understood their mood based on their gestures or facial expressions? If you have managed to do this, it means you could understand their body language. It refers to a variety of non-verbal cues that are communicated consciously and unconsciously. It includes everything associated with non-verbal communication.

Whereas, verbal communication is restricted to the words used while speaking.

When your non-verbal cues aren't in sync with the verbal ones, it creates discord between what you are saying. For instance, a smile is a pleasant facial expression that sends positive communication. However, a frown conveys anger or even discomfort. Now, if you are frowning while complimenting someone, it sends an ambiguous message. The different non-verbal cues that comprise your body language include facial expressions, tone of voice, hand gestures, and overall mannerisms. While looking at all this, you gain access to more information about what the person is saying along with their feelings.

Importance of Body Language

Why is it important to understand body language? The answer to this is based on the 7/38/55% communication rule developed in the 1960s by Albert Mehrabian, a psychology professor at the University of California. As per his research, the spoken word is believed to communicate only 7% of the total message. The tone of the voice used communicates around 38% of the total message while body language accounts for 55%. Since we convey a lot using our body language cues, understanding it is necessary if you want to become a better communicator. It also helps obtain better insight into what others are actually saying. Here are all the different benefits associated with understanding body language.

Learning to read someone's body language makes it easier to interpret their mood and emotions. It also gives better insight into what they're thinking or feeling. This information makes it easier to ensure you respond appropriately.

Learning to read body language enables you to build trust in relationships. Nonverbal cues can be used consciously to ensure that you are open and honest while communicating.

You can also learn to use different types of non-verbal cues to ensure that you portray confidence. This, in turn, helps make a good impression that goes a long way in establishing helpful relationships.

Body Language Habits to Avoid

When it comes to resolving a problem, understanding the root cause is necessary to ensure that you apply the right solution. Before you learn about which body language habits to avoid, it is important to understand how they are developed in the first place.

When it comes to understanding body language, it all starts with touch. Touch is an important part of the human experience. Whether it is a hug, kiss, or even a handshake, these are all gestures that help create a positive emotional feeling.

The human body likes to be touched and it does not like being stressed. Whenever you are stressed, your need for human touch increases. This probably is not the best choice of words, but this is how it works. If there is an internal increase in the level of stress, external stimulation in the form of touch helps. This is one of the reasons why people usually opt for movement in one form or another when they're anxious. Whether it is biting nails, rubbing their hands, or fidgeting, these are all results of self-stimulation. This is basic physiology at play when it comes to body language.

Constant Fidgeting

As mentioned, the human body loves stimulation regardless of whether it is sensory or cognitive. Fidgeting is a built-in stress pacification system for your body. It helps reduce the negative stimulus (that is social stress) by looking for a positive stimulus (that is sensory stimulation). This essentially means that the more you fidget, the greater the stress of nervousness you are expressing. To ensure that you are not constantly fidgeting in social settings, it's important to pay attention to your body language whenever you experience stress. Consciously notice what your arms and feet are doing. When you know you are stressed and further are aware of the reasons for it, taking corrective action becomes easier.

Slouching or Poor Posture

Your body posture conveys what you are feeling in a given moment. Certain postures convey confidence while others show weakness. You might have heard that slouching is not good. Well, why? Have you ever wondered why animals try to bring themselves up to the full height when confronted by a predator? This is to make themselves seem bigger and stronger than they are. On the other hand, slouching makes anyone seem small and weak. When you slouch, pressure is placed on the lumbar spine, which results in stretching the muscles in the lower back. This posture might feel good immediately but in the long run, it causes problems. When you slouch, it shows that you are anxious, nervous, worried, or weak. Well, this might not be the message you would want to convey in a social setting.

Rubbing Your Neck

Rubbing or massaging the neck is an instinctual stress-relieving exercise. The neck is home to a variety of blood vessels, nerves, and muscles. When stressed, they all tighten up. Rubbing your neck is a straightforward means to relieve stress. However, this gesture conveys a message that you are uncomfortable or anxious. The next time you feel an urge to rub your neck, ask yourself why you are experiencing an urge to do so.

Brushing Your Thighs

Have you ever noticed that nervous people tend to brush their thighs? As with the neck, even the thighs are home to a variety of sensory receptors due to their higher skin surface area. So, rubbing this region helps calm the body and is a self-pacifying behavior.

Rolling Your Eyes

Rolling your eyes is not only off-putting but is a major social faux pas that must be avoided. From an evolutionary perspective, the irises of the eyes helped communicate intention between members of a tribe. It is an intention-based signaling mechanism. Prolonged staring usually means that one person wants to communicate with the other. The simple action over the years in the form of basic communication has evolved and resulted in basic standards we still follow today. Now, let's get back to eye rolling. This simple gesture throws all the evolutionary standards out of the window. It is not only passive-aggressive but seems to convey disinterest, irritation, annoyance, and a variety of other emotions in different settings.

No Eye Contact

The lack of eye contact usually conveys a negative message. A lot of eye movement or the lack of it altogether indicates disinterest and distraction. We also avoid eye contact when we feel uncomfortable, guilty, or are trying to hide something. All in all, avoiding eye contact sends a poor message.

Biting Your Fingernails

Did you know that the act of biting fingernails has a specific word for it? This condition is technically described as onychophagia. It is usually caused by the urge to soothe yourself when you feel uncomfortable, anxious, stressed, or worried. The tips of your fingers are filled with sensory receptors. Therefore, biting or pinching them increases the pressure on them, which reduces stress. As mentioned, your body hates stress and likes to soothe itself. Nail biting is a self-soothing mechanism that reduces stress. It's important to avoid this behavior because fingernails that are torn or damaged in any form can be off-putting to others.

Readjusting Your Posture

You might have seen people readjust their position regardless of whether it is on social media or the television. This is not only quite common but is difficult to pick up on as well. Most tend to continuously readjust their posture whenever they are experiencing uncomfortable emotions. Whether it is stress, anxiety, or an uncomfortable situation, readjusting your posture is a response to it. Whenever you experience the urge to change your position or posture, especially during a conversation, it's a sign that you are anxious, stressed, or experiencing an uncomfortable emotion.

Crossing Your Arms

One of the most basic forms of negative body language is crossed arms. It is a classic sign and should be avoided. When you cross your arms, it shows that you have closed yourself off to the world and are not interested in whatever the other person is saying.

Intruding by Leaning Forward

It's an automatic response to lean forward whenever something interests us. For instance, you might notice that couples usually lean towards each other when on a date and are seated across the table. To a certain extent, it is a desirable posture. However, leaning forward too much can be considered to be an invasion of someone else's personal space. On the other hand, if you notice the language of powerful people, you will notice they slightly lean backward. This means they give the other person a chance to come to them. This also communicates value and influence.

Negative Expressions

Body language is not just limited to your posture or hand placement. It also includes your facial expressions. There are a variety of negative facial expressions that you must avoid during conversations. For instance, flared nostrils show disapproval or aggression. It also conveys a message that you are judging the other person. Pursing your lips displays displeasure. Similarly, confusion, anger, and disagreement are conveyed when you frown. Different negative facial expressions convey unhelpful attitudes and emotions. Displaying them can be off-putting for the other person, especially in a social setting.

Reading Body Language

In this section, let's look at some simple suggestions that can be used to read body language signals. By familiarizing yourself with them, it becomes easier to understand what others are saying. You can also use it for self-introspection to get a better understanding of your body language. This is especially helpful if you want to change your body language for the better.

Eyes

The eyes are the windows of the soul and play the most important role in nonverbal communication. When you maintain eye contact, it shows interest. When it is maintained for longer than needed, it becomes intimidating and threatening. The lack of eye contact indicates discomfort, distraction, or even a lie. Frequent blinking indicates that you are upset or uncomfortable while the lack of it becomes intimidating. When you are excited or attracted to something or someone, your pupils become dilated. A negative mood or anger is conveyed when your pupils become small or constricted.

Arms

Your arms are also an important part of non-verbal communication and body language. Those who usually keep their arms close to their body want to draw less attention to themselves. Crossing your arms indicates being closed off. It also indicates self-protection and defensiveness to a certain extent.

Facial Expressions

Our facial expressions are usually an unconscious reaction and they reveal a lot of information about what we are thinking. There are no global standards for it but some expressions indicate different emotions. The most common emotions you can recognize by facial expressions are sadness, happiness, fear, confusion, anger, excitement, and contempt.

Hands and Fingers

Hands and fingers are usually used for expressing a variety of emotions. Whether it is an obscene gesture or excitement conveyed by a clapping of hands, there is a lot they cover. A universal sign of approval is to give a thumbs-up. Anxiety or boredom are conveyed when your hands are clasped behind your back. Tapping your fingers rapidly expresses frustration or irritation. When you stand with your hands on your hips, it indicates that you are in control or it can also be interpreted as a sign of aggression. A clenched fist indicates solidarity or anger.

Feet and Legs

You might not have realized but your feet and legs also convey a lot of information about your mood and feelings. When you stand with both your feet pointed in a V-shape toward the person you are interacting with, it shows interest. When your feet are pointed away from the said person, it shows a lack of interest. Crossed legs also convey disinterest.

Mouth

One of the most important signs of body language is exhibited by your mouth. For instance, a smile can show your happiness and approval. Insecurity or worry is conveyed when you bite your lower lip. Covering the mouth is one of the most common ways in which a genuine reaction such as a smile or a smirk is often suppressed. Annoyance, disapproval, and distrust are usually conveyed by pursed lips.

Torso

An open and erect posture shows confidence and it also shows you are paying attention to the other person. On the other hand, crossed arms are often considered to be a closed body posture. When you slouch, it usually indicates disinterest or boredom.

Improve Your Body Language

Even if you have been making any of the above-mentioned mistakes, the good news is that you have complete control over fixing this immediately. With a little conscious effort and consistency, you can improve your body language. Doing so will not only improve your overall ability to communicate effectively with others but ensure you can develop better relationships too. Here are some simple suggestions that will come in handy.

Starts With Awareness

If you want to improve your body language the precondition to it is self-awareness. You must become aware of your current style of nonverbal communication, especially body language. A straightforward means of doing this is through self-introspection. Take some time and think about any social gathering or a meeting you attended recently. Now, think about how you conducted yourself not just physically but emotionally too. Think about your reaction to any information you received or how you felt about the overall situation. Regardless of whether it's a personal or professional gathering, understanding how you present yourself is necessary.

While doing this, think of all the gestures you usually use, your posture, facial expressions, and energy levels. If you are not yet sure how you present yourself, talking to your close friends and loved ones will offer the needed insight. Perhaps you have a nervous tic of tapping your feet without conscious thought. Or, maybe you hesitate to make eye contact. Whatever it is, make a note of all the things you do and areas where there is scope for improvement. After this, move on and try to improve your body language.

Make Eye Contact

Body language and non-verbal communication cannot exist without each other. Whenever you are communicating with someone, ensure that you focus on their eyes. Eyes communicate in a language that is more powerful and effective than words can ever be. They also reveal the truth. Maintaining appropriate and healthy eye contact is needed. This doesn't mean you stare without blinking. When you avoid eye contact, it shows that you are not paying attention or have something to hide. Instead, focus on maintaining pleasant and affirmative eye contact. If you want to work on this, the best thing you can do is to stand in front of a mirror and maintain eye contact with your reflection. Do this and have a full-blown conversation with your reflection. After all, practice is needed for improving yourself.

Smile

The easiest way to improve your overall body language is to smile pleasantly. It doesn't mean you need to have a fake smile plastered on your face. When you have a pleasant smile, it shows you're confident and comfortable with yourself and the situation. A calm smile has an immediate effect on those around you as well. Have you ever noticed that you automatically smile when someone smiles at you? Even if you don't know the other person, this is a knee-jerk reaction. It helps reassure others and make them comfortable.

Overall Energy

Your energy that's projected is equally important when it comes to your body language. For instance, if you seem stiff and formal at a social gathering, it can be off-putting. Understand that people are drawn to positive energy. This is one of the reasons we usually approach those who radiate positivity. If you can think of anyone in your immediate circle that oozes positivity, try spending more time with them. You can start mimicking or modeling their body language to help you radiate positive energy.

Project Confidence

If you want to become good at talking to anyone, the first thing you need to work on is projecting confidence. You can do this by focusing on your body language. Even if you don't feel too confident right now, you can learn. In the meanwhile, the concept of fake it till you make it works well. Simple changes can be made to your body language to communicate confidence. For instance, standing up straight and maintaining an open posture shows you are confident in your skin. Similarly, keeping your chin up and making eye contact toward the person you are talking to conveys confidence. On the other hand, not making eye contact, crossing your arms, hunching or slouching, crossing your legs, and fidgeting conveys a lack of confidence. It is easier to talk to someone when you project confidence. By consciously instilling positive changes to your body language, you can improve your confidence too.

Techniques to Use

Here are some helpful techniques you can utilize to improve your non-verbal communication.

Soften

Soften is the acronym for a communication technique that stands for smile, open, forward lean, time, eye contact, and nod. Following this technique is bound to instantly improve your non-verbal communication. Let's see what each of the ingredients of this acronym means. You must always smile at the person talking to you. Ensure that your posture, as well as facial expression, conveys openness toward the speaker. When you lean slightly forward toward the speaker, it shows interest in the conversation and that you are listening. When someone is talking, give them your time and do not interrupt. Maintaining eye contact is needed to ensure you convey the message you are actively listening to them. Also, nodding occasionally shows acknowledgment.

Mirroring

Mirroring is an excellent technique to make sure others feel comfortable around you. Have you ever noticed that when two people share a bond, they unknowingly mimic each other's behaviors? You can make yourself more approachable and amicable by mirroring. It refers to mimicking the body language displayed by the person you are talking to. From their facial expressions to body posture and gestures, mimicking such body language makes it easier for others to relate to you. It also increases their overall comfort level. While mirroring, ensure that you don't make it too obvious. If the other person feels as if you are copying every movement they make, it can be unsettling and this technique will backfire.

Modeling

Another effective means to use your body language to set the tone of interaction or conversation is known as modeling. It is a simple means to get others to mirror your body language. It is especially effective when used to introduce more positive energy into a room or a conversation. For instance, if the mood seems rather depressed, modeling positive body language such as a smile and open posture will make others do the same.

Summary

Let's quickly summarize the key points that were discussed in this chapter:

- In order to improve your communication skills, you will need to ensure that your body language is sending the correct information.
- Body language is any nonverbal message, this includes the following: facial expressions, tone of voice, gestures, etc.
- There are several common bad body language habits that can take place during a conversation; these bad habits (e.g. rolling your eyes, poor posture, etc.) will limit your ability to connect with others.

- You can also use body language to understand how others think or feel; there are several examples discussed in this chapter (e.g. if someone has their arms crossed they are most likely not interested in having a conversation).
- To overcome bad body language, you first need to become self-aware of what patterns you are exhibiting; once you have identified the body language that you want to correct, you need to apply

the relevant techniques (e.g. soften, modeling, mirroring) to fix it.

Call to Action

Bad body language is an example of a bad habit. When a trigger occurs, you end up responding with the appropriate bad body language. This means that if you want to fix bad body language, you need to apply the same solution for breaking bad habits. Therefore, we will have the same call to action from the previous chapter with some minor changes.

Track Your Bad Body Language

- Go to your personal device, access the app store, and find a habit tracker app that works for you. Alternatively, you can set-up a manual journal on either your personal device or on a written notepad.

- The next time you exhibit a behavior that you dislike, capture it in either the app of your choice or in your journal. Make sure to include details from the habit loop: the trigger, the behavior, and the reward. Continue to log these details each time it happens. Eventually, you will notice a pattern will emerge. At this point, you have identified the bad body language habit.

Replace Bad Body Language & Continue to Track

- Once you have identified the bad body language habit, you will need to disrupt it. Write down what the replacement behavior (e.g. soften, model, mirror) will be, and how you plan to reward yourself for the new behavior. Each time the trigger occurs, apply the new behavior and the new reward. Remember, without a reward, it will be harder for a new habit to stick.

- Keep track of both the old and new behavior. If you are consistent and patient enough. You will eventually see a reduction in the old behavior and an increase in the new behavior. The more you eliminate the bad body language habits and continue to replace them with better ones the more confident you will look.

Chapter 4
How to Start a Conversation

Have you observed someone who has the ability to start a conversation with anyone? Do you look at them and wonder how they do it? If you don't feel capable or struggle with starting a conversation, you already know how tough it can be. Well, the good news is, that change is the only constant in life. It means you have the power to learn to start a conversation with others. This can be the toughest aspect of socializing. However, not making the first move in life can be a big mistake. You don't have to wait for someone else to start a conversation with you. Instead, you can learn to do it yourself. This doesn't mean you should always be the first one to initiate a conversation. However, once you learn to start and maintain conversations you will notice a positive change in several aspects. For instance, networking becomes easier. Similarly, you can also notice progress in your love life.

Whenever you are learning something new, focusing on all the different benefits it offers is necessary. Understanding why it is beneficial to learn to start a conversation will increase your motivation to do this. When you can initiate conversations with people you don't know, it shows you have an aura around you that others want to be part of. It makes you seem more approachable. It also enables you to meet new people and develop a network of friends or even peers, which leads to more experiences as well as knowledge sharing.

The ability to have a good time with anyone is a worthy trait. When you can strike up a conversation with others it shows them that you are interested in getting to know them. This by itself helps break the ice for building better relationships. It also teaches you more about how others approach social situations. When the number of positive relationships increases in your life, your overall sense of happiness increases. It also increases your self-esteem and confidence.

There are four simple rules you must not forget when it comes to initiating conversations.

The first rule is to always be polite. Within context, don't forget that you are in the company of strangers, and you shouldn't make anyone feel uncomfortable. First impressions matter and therefore, always be polite. The second rule is to keep the conversation light. You don't have to emotionally unload your burdens onto someone you have just met. Do not share personal details within the first five minutes of meeting someone. Instead, keep the conversation light and avoid launching into a heartfelt rant or a sob story. The third rule is to have fun and relax. The final rule is to always be honest. You don't have to pretend to be someone else. Others can also tell when you are lying. When you are genuine and honest, it increases the chance that others are willing to talk to you. This, in turn, keeps the conversation flowing.

Start a Conversation With Anyone

Imagine that you are at a conference, party, or even the local park and you see someone that you want to talk with. It can be someone you noticed for the first time, a potential client for your business, or someone you have a romantic interest in. You can either maintain your distance and avoid the person entirely or take the initiative to strike up a conversation with them. This probably sounds simple, but in that instance, do you know what to say to this person? Do you start worrying that you don't know what to talk about? Does thinking about all this give you anxiety and scare you from even making the first move?

You don't need to be in this situation ever again. You can start a conversation with anyone and at any time. You can also do this gracefully. In this section, let's look at some simple and practical suggestions that can be easily followed to help initiate conversations with pretty much anyone.

Rapport Across the Room

You can build rapport with others without even saying a word. It can be something as simple as a reciprocated smile or even eye contact. When you acknowledge someone's presence before approaching and talking to them, it makes the conversation easier to start. It also goes a long way in making the introduction much easier than it would have been without the rapport. For instance, if there is someone you admire at the party, you make eye contact with them and if it is reciprocated, why don't you go ahead and introduce yourself? This rapport essentially acts as a cue to start the conversation.

One thing you must understand is just because you are trying to build a rapport across the room it doesn't mean everyone is going to flock to you. It still means you'll have to make a little effort and initiate the conversation.

Mindset Matters

Your mindset matters in all aspects of life and starting a conversation with someone is not an exception. Having the right mindset makes it easier to start a conversation with a stranger. When starting a conversation with a stranger, your thoughts consider all the unknown variables. Such thoughts simply increase fear and make you hesitant. The simplest way to change your mindset is to let go of any worrying thoughts that bring you down when you are trying to approach someone. One thing you should not forget in life is that unless you take a risk you will not get a reward. If you are worried that the person you have approached will give you the cold shoulder or will reject you, ask yourself, "What is the worst that will happen?" It might mean you will not get to have a conversation with them. That's likely the worst-case scenario.

Common Ground

One of the best ways to start a conversation is by identifying a common interest or trait. This is an icebreaker that makes it easier to start conversing. If you notice something in common with a stranger, use it as an opening line. Perhaps it is an article of clothing that supports a sports team that you like, a tattoo on their body, or it could also be a specific brand of the clothing. You can use it to start a conversation. A conversation that starts with a similar interest or is based on shared interests is more engaging. It also increases the chances of establishing a genuine connection with the other person. Remember that the world is filled with different people who have varying ideas and opinions. So, look for some common ground and base the conversation around it.

A Common Topic Helps

A straightforward yet effective means to start a conversation with anyone is to comment on a common topic. It probably sounds silly but it is effective. There are several things that you share in common with the other person when you exist in the same space. The most common topics you can start talking about include the weather and traffic. Is it extremely hot? Is the weather frosty and unbearably cold? Perhaps it's been raining endlessly? Or maybe it's a beautiful day out there! Whatever it is, you can start a conversation by sharing your delight or frustration about the weather conditions. Do not shift into a full-blown technical mode and explain the weather. Instead, it should just be a passing comment. Chances are the person you are trying to talk to will reciprocate and reply.

For instance, those living in a metropolitan city are usually frustrated about the traffic conditions. This topic of traffic can be a conversation starter. If everyone experiences the craziness of the traffic on their way to or from work then it's a common topic that can be discussed. Maybe you can share a secret shortcut or two that bypasses some of the traffic. Make the most of this opportunity and say something about it. Apart from this, simply look around your environment and look for something common you share with this stranger. Whether it is a beautiful garden or a child playing recklessly, you can simply comment about this and initiate a conversation. That said, ensure that the situation is apt before you try to initiate a conversation. For instance, if someone seems to be in a hurry to get somewhere and you are trying to initiate a conversation about the weather, it will backfire.

Concentrate on Something Pleasant

If you are struggling to find something meaningful to talk about, then focus on something pleasant. For instance, if you are at a party, saying something as simple as, "Wow, this is a great turnout for this event," or "These canapés taste amazing," can do the trick! You can find something positive to talk about in any situation. You simply need to look for it and then express it. Saying something negative might initiate a conversation but it is too risky. For instance, you are at a conference and start a conversation with someone new by saying, "that keynote address was too boring." However, it turns out the person you just told this to is the keynote speaker's partner. At this point, you just ended any chance of having a good conversation. To avoid getting embroiled in controversies and to ensure you do not start a conversation on the wrong foot, avoid any criticism as a conversation starter.

Ask for Assistance

In some situations, asking for assistance from someone else can also be a conversation starter. Whether it is help reaching a top shelf or asking someone to help find something you misplaced. However, it is unlikely that you have such situations in all scenarios. If an opportunity presents itself, go ahead and take it. It's okay to ask others for help. Ensure that your request is genuine and something you cannot do. Similarly, you can also offer assistance if you see someone struggling. Once again this might not be applicable in all situations but offering assistance, especially to someone you are keen on talking to, is a great chance. Before you ask or offer assistance, ensure that you are not excessive or intrusive. If it looks like you have eavesdropped or pushed yourself into an ongoing conversation, it will backfire.

Develop Confidence

How you present yourself matters because it determines how others respond to you. When you exude confidence, it becomes easier for others to talk to you. This can be the most challenging aspect of initiating a conversation because you might not feel confident. You're probably wondering how others will respond to you, whether your approach is right, or if you are saying the right things. These thoughts can quickly erode your self-confidence. On the other hand, when you exude self-confidence, it shows you are in control of the situation. If you doubt your worth or think you are uninteresting, then it is time to fix this. The simplest means to do this is by taking some time for self-introspection and making a note of different reasons why you are an interesting person. If you think you don't have any exciting stories to share, why don't you look for something from the past that shows you are interesting. Understand that you are worth talking to. If you think you are uninteresting or that you are not worth it, others will also sense it. It is okay to have setbacks and weaknesses but not playing to your strengths is a mistake.

Summary

Let's quickly summarize the key points that were discussed in this chapter:

- In order to improve your communication skills, you will need to ensure that you can comfortably start a conversation with anyone.

- Being able to start a conversation with anyone will allow you to meet new people, network with others, strengthen bonds, and build meaningful relationships.

- The key to starting a conversation is to not overthink the situation and to simply focus on commonalities (e.g. ask them a question that they can easily answer, comment on a sports team that they are brandishing on their shirt, comment on something happening at the event your both attending, etc.)

Call to Action

Let's have a look at the call to action that will help you start a conversation.

Prepare in Advance

- If you know you are going to have to go to an event or venue where you need to initiate conversations, the best thing you can do is prepare in advance. Recognize your audience (the people attending the event or venue). Think of the relevant commonalities you both can discuss. Do a little research and have a couple of topics that you can reference as an icebreaker. This will help get the conversation started.

Chapter 5
Master Small Talk

If you want to become a good conversationalist, then mastering small talk is a must. Learning to become good at small talk not only offers personal gains, but will come in handy in your professional life too. Have you ever been in a situation where you are talking to someone and run out of things to talk about? You end up in an awkward silence hoping that some sort of distraction will appear? Do such situations make you want to wish for a secret escape? Well, you can stop worrying, as this chapter will help you master the art of small talk.

What is Small Talk?

What does small talk mean? It's a type of conversation that usually takes place between strangers. It allows for the individuals to gauge each other in a light and polite way. It is a simple yet effective means to connect with others. When done properly, you will end up with friends, colleagues, business associates, and relationships that will last a lifetime. Small talk helps transform non-familiar relationships into familiar ones. When you use it constructively, it makes it easier to get through your day and interact with new people. You can also use it for presenting your ideas and building an impressive structure for future communication.

Small talk is the perfect filler in conversations. Usually, silence in a conversation is considered to be awkward and uncomfortable. If even after a couple of minutes you seem to have lost the conversational thread, you can regain it using small talk. If it feels like the other person isn't interested in talking any further, give them the space to leave.

Another benefit of small talk is that it can prevent conversations from abruptly ending. When a conversation abruptly ends, it can feel like a rejection to the other person. To ensure this doesn't happen, you can use small talk. Small talk helps shift the focus from a serious topic to something lighter. This, in turn, makes it easier to mitigate any awkwardness and can allow you to end any conversation on a pleasing note.

Benefits of Small Talk

Even though it is known as small talk, when used properly, the benefits it offers are significant. Some of the advantages of engaging in small talk are as follows.

Small talk is a great way to offer information to others in a brief span of time. It also enables you to evaluate the atmosphere. You can use it to understand more about the person you are trying to talk to. It allows you to create a lasting impression on someone.

Chatting with strangers or even acquaintances can be a source of new ideas and inspiration. When you talk to someone, chances are you are purely focused on impressing them. This means you are thinking of new topics, solutions to problems, or other similar things to find some common ground. In a way, this enables you to think outside the box.

Whether it is a relationship with your close friend or even partner, all this started somewhere at some time with small talk. Every friendship requires a beginning. You never know, you might end up meeting someone new and create a lifelong bond with them purely based on small talk. So, stop ignoring it and instead, focus on making the most of every opportunity you get to talk to others.

Learning The Art of Small Talk

Small talk is the best way to improve your socializing skills. If you believe these skills are a little rusty or you need to hone them, there is no time like the present to get started. Regardless of whether it's a cocktail party or a business meeting, making small talk is not always as easy as it sounds. Talking with a stranger can at times become mildly painful or extremely awkward. However, just like anything else in life, you need to continue practicing to improve and eventually you will master small talk. The only thing you need to remember is you don't have to reach for perfection. Keep working on it and you'll be able to reap the benefits in no time.

IFR Method

Here is an effective means to keep the conversation interesting and well balanced. This method is known as IFR and it is an acronym for inquire, follow up, and relate. This method ensures that you don't end up asking too many questions in a row or talk too much about yourself.

While using this method, you need to start by asking a sincere question, which is the first step — inquire. After this, you'll have to ask a follow-up question, which is the second step. The third step is to share a little bit of information about yourself that relates to what has been shared by the other person. After this, you can start the loop again by asking another sincere question.

For instance, if you meet someone at a party who turns out to be a filmmaker, you could probably ask them about the kind of movies they make. After they answer, you can ask them a follow-up question about any specific interest they have or anything associated with the movies they made.

And finally, you simply need to say something, which is in sync with the answer given by them.

ARE Method

Just like the above-mentioned IFR technique, there is another method you can use to facilitate small talk known as ARE. This acronym stands for anchor, reveal, and encourage. Here are the steps you need to follow.

The first step is to create an "anchor." An anchor essentially means you have to observe a reality that is mutual or shared. It can be about something you are either experiencing or witnessing. Depending on the setting of the encounter, this will vary. For instance, if you bump into someone at the grocery store and notice that you are both buying the same product, this can be your anchor to start the conversation.

The second step is "reveal." In this, you need to say something that connects to the anchor mentioned in the previous step. For instance, at the grocery store, if you notice that the watermelons are on sale, you can remark about it. Or perhaps you can also use another story or a similar incident to keep the conversation going.

The last but definitely not the least step is to "encourage" the conversation. To do this, you can ask an open-ended question or something more specific that is associated with the second step. For instance, if you are at the grocery store you can encourage the conversation by asking them about something general or specific such as "what do you think about these melons?" Or "what do you think about this deal?"

Summary

Let's quickly summarize the key points that were discussed in this chapter:

- In order to improve your communication skills, you will need to ensure that you master the art of small talk.
- Small talk is a pivotal tool that can be used for any conversation, it provides the following benefits: it helps keep the conversation flowing smoothly, it allows you to gauge other people, and it can help convert relationships from non-familiar to familiar.
- Mastering the art of small talk requires the utilization of the following techniques: IFR (Inquire, Follow-up, and Relate) & ARE (Anchor, Reveal, and Encourage).

Chapter 6
Listen, Listen, Listen

Listening is something that we all do daily. A reasonable assumption is that we should all be good at it. Unfortunately, most of us are poor listeners. The average person manages to retain only about 50% of any conversation. This further drops to 25% within 48 hours. It essentially means that we end up retaining only about 1/4th of the information actually conveyed to us. Poor listening skills affect a significant percentage of the population. It results in errors, missed opportunities, miscommunication, misunderstandings, and even damaged relationships. However, all this can be changed once you learn to become an active listener. Now, it is time to understand that a conversation is not just about talking. Instead, there needs to be a listener as well. If not, wouldn't we all just be talking over each other? In this chapter, you will learn about the different types of listening, the common barriers to active listening, and how to become an active listener.

Types of Listening

It probably sounds surprising, but there is more than one type of listening. There are two types, active and passive listening.

Passive listening, as the name suggests, refers to hearing something or someone without giving them your full attention. It is usually one-sided communication when the speaker hardly or doesn't even receive any feedback. The chances of the speaker being heard are quite limited here. It doesn't require any effort and the passive listener usually ends up missing out on important parts of the conversation because they weren't paying attention. Have you ever absentmindedly nodded your head or maintained eye contact with someone even when you are not fully listening to them? Chances are you were lost in a daydream or were thinking of something else. If yes, then you were a passive listener.

On the other hand, active listening, as the name suggests, refers to actively listening to what is being said. In this, the listener's focus is fully directed toward what is being said. Such listeners usually offer feedback intermittently or after the speaker is done talking. When you pay 100% attention to what is being said, your ability to understand and grasp the information shared also increases. It reduces the chances of miscommunication and misunderstandings.

Apart from all this, it ensures that you have fully understood what is being said.

Poor Listening Habits

Different habits prevent active listening. They are as follows.

Partial Listening

Most of us are partial listeners. Have you ever been on a phone call with someone while being preoccupied with another activity? Perhaps you were flipping through pages of a magazine, reading your emails, or even scrolling through social media while someone else was talking to you. In that instance, you were not fully listening to what is being said. Instead, you were preoccupied. Multitasking in any form, while someone else is talking to you, makes you a partial listener.

Bias or Judgment

There are instances when the listener might have certain biases against the speaker. Or, perhaps they have already judged them before they have uttered a word. Such initial biases and judgments prevent you from fully understanding what the person is saying. Perhaps you have judged them based on their dressing style, mannerisms, or even body language. This preconceived notion you have in your head will cloud everything else they say and prevent you from fully and truly understanding what is being said.

Any Negativity

As with a bias or judgment, if you have any negativity toward the speaker, it influences your ability to fully understand what is being said. This is because you already do not approve of the speaker or their ideas. Due to this, there is always distortion in the message being conveyed which increases the chances of it being misinterpreted and misunderstood. For instance, you and the speaker might have extremely different ideologies. This will clash with everything you believe in. Due to this, the chances are that you will end up disagreeing with what is being said. Similarly, the chances of you not paying full attention to what is being said are also high.

No Confidence

The lack of confidence can also get in the way of active listening. If you already have a strong notion about yourself that you will not understand what is being said, the willingness to fully listen will reduce. After all, what is the point of trying if you already think you will not get it?

Inability to Tolerate

There are instances when some are unwilling to listen to what the others have to say because they are extremely excited to share their insights or have questions they want to be answered. Regardless of what it is, if you are constantly interrupting the other person, you cannot fully understand what they're saying. This is one of the reasons why you are supposed to be 100% fully present in the conversation and simply listen when someone is speaking. If you keep interrupting the speaker, you'll never understand what they're trying to say.

Benefits of Active Listening

If you are not a good listener, it is never too late to become one. As with anything else in life, learning a little about the benefits you can gain will increase your motivation to make this change. In the section, let's look at all the different benefits associated with active listening.

Recall Information

The ability to remember and recall precise information increases when you are actively listening to the speaker. If you are distracted by something else, you cannot be fully present in the moment. This prevents you from listening to what is being said. For instance, if the speaker is offering guidance or instructions about doing a certain task and you zone out, you will not know what needs to be done. To ensure you do not get stuck in such situations, be 100% present when someone else is talking to you.

Resolve Problems

Your problem-solving abilities improve when you are actively listening to others. It helps detect any obstacles or issues others are experiencing. This allows you to help rectify their problems. When you are simply listening to the information being conveyed, it will make you more aware of the problems. The sooner you recognize the problem, the quicker it can be resolved.

Building Connections

When you are fully listening to someone, it automatically encourages them to reciprocate. Wouldn't you be more inclined to hear someone out if they were patiently hearing you out? Extending this courtesy to others helps create stronger relationships. It also fosters healthy conversations. When your willingness to listen to what others are saying and your ability to understand them improves, you can be more empathetic to them. This simple act by itself goes a long way in improving your relationships. It also makes it easier to communicate with others.

Improve Your Knowledge

You cannot learn unless you are listening to what others are sharing. For instance, you are at a business seminar and are being guided about valuable business processes, but you choose not to listen to it because you dislike the speaker. Now you may have missed out on important information that could have helped you and your business. All this can be circumvented if you were just listening. When you actively listen to what is being said by others around you, it offers valuable insights into different aspects of life. Remember that no two individuals are alike and therefore, we all differ in how we think, act, and behave. By observing others and listening to what they are saying, you can improve your knowledge.

Building Trust

It becomes easier to build trust in a relationship when you let someone else talk without any interruptions or disruptions. If the speaker is trying to convey something and you constantly interrupt them, they will lose interest in the conversation. They might not even approach you, even if they want to share something in the future. To ensure this doesn't happen, you need to be actively listening to what is being said. When you learn to listen without interrupting the speaker, they will feel more comfortable talking to you. This also helps deepen the bonds and improves the trust in the relationship. Regardless of whether it is a personal or professional relationship, this benefit comes in handy at all levels.

Avoiding Misunderstandings

A common reason why misunderstandings occur is that most of us listen only to give a reply. We are not listening to understand. Instead, we are calculating and formulating our responses. Due to this, disagreements, arguments, and misunderstandings are created in relationships. When left unregulated these things can quickly break even the strongest of relationships. The simplest way to avoid miscommunication and misunderstandings is to fully listen to what is being said. If you have any doubts or questions you believe need clarification, you can always ask the speaker after they have finished sharing. Isn't this a more effective and calmer means to resolve an issue instead of jumping to conclusions and misunderstanding what was said?

How to Become an Active Listener

Becoming an active listener and improving your listening skills are beneficial to all relationships in your life. Some people are naturally good listeners while others need to train themselves to become better. With a little practice and consistency, you can become an active listener. Here are some suggestions that will come in handy along the way.

No Distractions

The first rule of active listening is to ensure there are no distractions. However, it's not just about focusing on external distractions. You must also get rid of internal distractions too. For now, let's focus on external distractions, as they are pretty easy to deal with. To avoid external distractions, you should avoid glancing at your phone, replying to emails, reading, or doing anything else while someone is talking to you. Do whatever is needed to ensure that you get rid of these extractions. Instead, focus only on what is being said.

Avoiding internal distractions takes more practice. If you are not used to being a good listener, chances are you're constantly distracted by different thoughts running in your head. It is time to quieten these thoughts and instead focus only on the conversation. If it feels like your focus is wavering, consciously bring it back to what is being shared. This is something that takes effort and practice. Once you learn to dial down the internal noise, your ability to fully understand what the other people are saying increases. It makes you more mindful as well.

Content and Context Matter

It's incredibly important that you carefully listen to the words that the other person is saying. It's not just the content but you should also listen to the context in which these words are being said. At times, words and ideas are used to convey a different meaning when taken in a specific context. The words the other person says will help understand what they are talking about. However, by paying attention to the context, you can pick up some common themes or any underlying tones that aren't explicitly expressed. It's about fully listening to the words and ideas they have spoken in a context.

Body Language Matters

Always be mindful of your body language when you are listening to someone. Body language not only applies when you are the speaker, but when you are the listener as well. Your body language is incredibly powerful, and it can convey the message that you are either paying attention or are disinterested in what is being said. You will need to project body language that conveys that you are actively listening and are engaged in the conversation. The simplest way to do this is to ensure that your torso faces the speaker, and you are leaning toward them to a certain degree. Do not lean forward to the extent that you are intruding into their personal space. Remember, in the chapter about body language you were introduced to different techniques to project ideal body language? Well, now is the time to start using all of it. If you are listening, you can mirror the speaker's behavior to make them feel more comfortable.

Speaking of body language, you should ensure that you are maintaining sufficient eye contact without staring at the speaker. It's a bit much if you end up staring without blinking at the speaker. It can look aggressive. Ensure that you maintain a comfortable level of eye contact when they are speaking. If you are not maintaining a comfortable level of eye contact or refuse to make eye contact, the speaker will lose interest.

Notice Emotions

When someone is speaking, ensure that you pay attention to their emotions as well. You cannot do this unless you are fully engaged in the conversation. When you watch for the underlying emotions or the undercurrent, it gives you more information about what is being said. It also enables you to gain better insight into where the speaker is coming from. This makes it easier to talk to others. Most of us cannot robotically deliver information. We usually have emotions that guide the way. Noticing their emotions makes it easier to gauge the kind of response you should be giving. For instance, if someone seems sad, then grinning is a very bad idea. On the other hand, if they are sharing something exciting, a smile can be encouraging. This helps the conversation stay alive.

Encourage Verbal Cues

Verbal cues are extremely helpful and can be used for eliciting a reaction or response from the speaker. Saying, "yes," "I understand," or even "hmm" occasionally while someone else is talking shows that you are listening. You can also use other gestures such as an occasional nod or a smile to convey the same.

Apart from using verbal cues, you should also be attentive to any verbal cues you receive from the speaker. Perhaps they talk softly about a specific point or stress certain words. They might even use a different tone or pause between sentences while talking about something. All these cues show that the speaker wants you to pay extra attention to what is being said. If there is silence, they might be expecting a response from you, and in these instances, showing that you have understood what they said is sufficient. If you haven't fully understood what they're saying, move on to the next suggestion.

Paraphrasing Helps

Apart from encouraging verbal cues, paraphrasing information that the speaker conveys is also a great way to show that you are listening. Paraphrasing information shows the other person that you were listening. It also enables the speaker to know that you have understood exactly what they are saying. It allows you to clarify if you have any doubts or haven't fully understood something. In a casual conversation, clarifying what someone else has said helps demonstrate support as well as empathy. In a professional setting, paraphrasing information conveys that you have accurately understood what was being communicated.

Open-Ended Questions

Asking open-ended questions also helps eliminate any traces of confusion and offers more clarity. If you think you haven't fully understood what the other person is saying or require more clarity go ahead and ask questions. Doing this is perfectly normal and acceptable. However, ensure that the other person has stopped talking before you ask some questions. Do not interrupt them mid-sentence. Always politely wait to ask your question.

You can also demonstrate your interest in the conversation by asking open-ended questions. These questions give the speaker a chance to elaborate further upon what they have said. It also shows that you were actively listening to whatever they were saying until now. It helps create a better and more positive bond between you and the speaker.

No Judgment

If you want to become an active listener, ensure that you do not judge the other person. You'll need to remain open and listen to what they have to say. It doesn't matter whether you agree with them or not. Even if you strongly disagree with what they are saying, remember that your role is that of a listener. No one asked you for your opinions and thoughts. Do not offer unsolicited advice unless you are asked for it. If you have any questions, you can ask them and clarify what was said. However, keep an open mind to all that was said. Approach every conversation with an open mind and try to see where the other person is coming from.

Summary

Let's quickly summarize the key points that were discussed in this chapter:

- In order to improve your communication skills, you will need to become a better listener.
- There are two types of listening: active listening and passive listening.
- Passive listening is when a person does not actively engage in a conversation and only partially absorbs the message that is being sent.

- There are common barriers that prevent us from listening, they are the following: being distracted, choosing not to listen, biases that prevent us from listening to others, etc.

- Active listening is when a person fully commits to the conversation and is making sure that they absorb all of the information that is being communicated to them.

- The benefits of active listening are the following: you will remember information better, avoid misunderstandings, and build trust with others.

- To become a better listener, you have to be able to do the following: clear your mind from any biases, provide your full attention, read the other person's body language, and verify that you understood the message that is being relayed.

Call to Action

Poor listening is another example of a bad habit. When a trigger occurs, you end up responding with the appropriate bad listening habits that prevent you from fully absorbing the message. This means that if you want to fix your poor listening skills, you need to apply the same solution for breaking bad habits. Therefore, we will have the same call to action from the previous chapter with some minor changes.

Track Your Poor Listening Habits

- Go to your personal device, access the app store, and find a habit tracker app that works for you. Alternatively, you can set-up a manual journal on either your personal device or on a written notepad.

- The next time you exhibit a behavior that you dislike, capture it in either the app of your choice or in your journal. Make sure to include details from the habit loop: the trigger, the behavior, and the reward. Continue to log these details each time it happens. Eventually, you will notice a pattern will emerge. At this point, you have identified a poor listening habit.

Replace Poor Listening Habits & Continue to Track

- Once you have identified a poor listening habit, you will need to disrupt it. Write down what the replacement behavior (e.g. clear distractions, engage in the conversation, verify what you heard) will be, and how you plan to reward yourself for the new behavior. Each time the trigger occurs, apply the new behavior and the new reward. Remember, without a reward, it will be harder for a new habit to stick.

- Keep track of both the old and new behavior. If you are consistent and patient enough. You will eventually see a reduction in the old behavior and an increase in the new behavior. The more you eliminate poor listening skills and continue to replace them with active listening skills the better you will become at listening to others.

Chapter 7
The Start of Something Wonderful

A point that has been repeatedly stressed in this book is that improving your communication skills is needed for building and maintaining meaningful relationships. Well, what does a meaningful relationship even mean? A meaningful relationship is any relationship that is of great personal significance to you. It should be healthy, long lasting, based on mutual respect and care. In such relationships, the other person encourages, supports, and stands by you when needed. These individuals help you grow and become a better version of yourself. When all of the correct ingredients are present in a relationship, it automatically adds more value to your life.

The Value of Meaningful Relationships

A close relationship is nothing short of being truly magical. Humans are social animals and we thrive in groups. This group could be something you were born into or a group you created. Regardless of what it is, it is needed for your overall well-being and health. The power of healthy companionship can never be underestimated. Here are all the different benefits associated with developing and maintaining meaningful relationships in life.

Better Mental Health

The mental health benefits associated with deeper and meaningful relationships cannot be overlooked. It reduces stress, increases the happiness quotient, and makes life more enjoyable. Being your authentic self and obtaining acceptance for it is freeing. It also improves your sense of satisfaction and contentment when you start living life on your terms. Another wonderful thing about meaningful relationships is it reduces the feelings of loneliness. Loneliness can increase the risk of depression and other mental health problems. All this is replaced with positivity and happiness when you have deeper bonds.

A Source of Support

Whether it is a platonic, working, or romantic relationship, meaningful bonds become a source of support. The support obtained from such relationships is unlike any other. It gives you a more positive outlook toward yourself, others, and life in general. We are social creatures and the feelings of positivity increase when you have meaningful relationships. When you know there is someone you can rely on in your time of need, it becomes easier to get through challenges. A meaningful relationship helps obtain the support or help you desire in the form you need. It offers healthy encouragement too.

Self-Improvement

The motivation to work on yourself improves when you have meaningful relationships. Whether it is a colleague, partner, or a family member, the desire to make yourself better improves. The lack of meaningful relationships increases the risk of falling into self-serving patterns. When you are around others, especially people you love, it teaches you selflessness. It allows you to show compassion to others. Personal growth is important but it is not a simple process. It includes a variety of challenges. Usually, we are our worst critics and therefore, we are the reasons why we cannot move forward. When you know that you are loved, supported, and understood how you are, it gives you immense internal strength. When you know you have others to count on and that they have your back, it becomes easier to focus on improving yourself. It gives you the confidence to aim higher. Instead of worrying about your relationships, you will be more secure in them. All the extra energy that previously went toward worrying about relationships can be directed to something productive.

Value Addition

Meaningful and deep relationships lend a positive flavor to all your experiences. It essentially performs a value-addition function that improves your overall outlook toward life in general. Meaningful relationships add personal value to your life. Understand that this is not the same as self-esteem. Your self-esteem should always stem from the inside. However, when you know that you are appreciated by others and have meaningful relationships, it makes you feel good about yourself. It improves your sense of confidence and adds more happiness to your life.

We feel good about ourselves when we know we are needed. We feel even better when we can love someone and be loved in return. All these aspects have to be taken care of when you have meaningful relationships in life. It improves the overall quality of your life. In a way, meaningful relationships do this by taking care of your needs. When your basic needs are taken care of, the motivation, confidence, and strength needed to chase your dreams and goals become easier.

Being Authentic

We all wear different masks in life. These masks differ from one instance to another. Your work mask will be different from the one you wear while meeting an old acquaintance or when at a party. Why do we do this? We do this because we are trying to protect ourselves from judgment or any scrutiny. Wearing a mask is our answer to, "what would they think if they knew me?" Or, "what would others say if they knew who I am?" Every mask you wear is nothing but a persona, and it comes with its own set of rules and behavioral parameters. We do this to feel accepted. We need to feel a sense of belonging, and being accepted is a crucial psychological need. In fact, as per Maslow's hierarchy of needs, the need for love and belonging comes before self-esteem and other self-actualization needs. If wearing a mask is the best way to prevent judgment and increase the chances of being accepted, it obviously doesn't seem like a bad idea.

Unfortunately, we are all living in a world where we are told to be happy and at the same time, to fit in. This is a paradox. It is the paradox of trying to fit in while expressing our true selves. As mentioned, Maslow's hierarchy of needs suggests that having the respect of others and a sense of belongingness are prioritized over respecting our needs or self-esteem. It is important to understand that we also wear masks unknowingly. You might not even be aware that you are hiding from the world. In the end, wearing too many masks does more harm than good. Ultimately you will be left in a crisis where you are unable to understand who you truly are. By trying to protect yourself, you end up hurting your true self — due to the lack of authenticity.

Unless you are authentic or genuine, you cannot form true and meaningful connections. Any bond that is based on wearing a mask or not being your authentic self is bound to crumble sooner or later. There is only so much energy you have to keep up the act of being someone you are not. This is why you should try to be more authentic. When you are authentic, it means you can be your true self without any worries. When you are your true self and know that you are accepted unconditionally, it becomes a source of immense self-confidence. It also gives you incredible support. There is comfort in knowing that someone has got your back based on who you actually are as a person.

The decision to be yourself is not an easy one. It takes immense courage and internal strength. At times, it might feel as if you are walking naked in the middle of a battlefield. The mask might have given you a little confidence and power but it is not authentic. When you learn to be your true self, it automatically increases your self-esteem and confidence. In any relationship being authentic means being your true self. It means being true to your mindset, behaviors, actions, and your nature. It means you can stop doing or saying things because you believe others want you to or because society expects you to. Instead, it is about being in touch with your inner self.

Your self-confidence, self-esteem, sense of clarity, motivation, and inner peace increase when you are authentic. It makes it easier to accept yourself. This, in turn, means you stop judging others. It makes you more effective at everything you do regardless of whether it is a business meeting or a personal conversation. It reduces self-doubt and makes you more flexible, positive, and alive. It makes you happier, and finally, sets you free.

It is never too late to be your authentic self. You can increase your authenticity with a little extra effort. The first step you must focus on is improving your self-awareness. It is about knowing who you are right now, who your inner self is, and who you want to be. If you could be someone without any worry or judgment, who would you be? The answer will tell you about your true self. Learn to become a passive observer of your life and it will give you better insight into yourself. Reflect upon who you are or how you present yourself in different situations. Do you change your opinions, likes, preferences, and other facets of your personality, just to make a specific person or group like you? Do you keep changing this with every group you mingle with? If you are presenting multiple versions of yourself to different people, it means you're not being authentic. It causes a lot of confusion and internal chaos. The simplest way to stop doing this is by observing who you want to be and who you are right now.

There are different ways in which you can get to know yourself. Ultimately, it all boils down to knowing that you have the power to choose who you want to be from now on. Who you were in the past doesn't matter and who you are right now can be changed. You should only focus on who you want to be and if you ensure that it is your authentic self, the quality of your life will improve. From taking personality assessments to working with your close friends and loved ones, it will teach you more about yourself. Taking notes of things that make you happy and things that make you unhappy is a great place to start. It will give you better insight into who you are. Once you know who you are, it is simply time to let go of the masks and be this version.

It Is Okay to Be Vulnerable

You cannot have a deep relationship without being vulnerable. Regardless of whether it is a friendship, romantic interest, or any other relationship, vulnerability is what makes the bond authentic. It ensures that you are honest not just with each other but your overall self as well. It reduces misunderstandings, breaks down walls we have built around ourselves, and reduces the risk of miscommunication. Apart from all this, it ensures that you are being your authentic self. So, what does vulnerability mean? It essentially refers to a willingness to risk revealing your weaknesses and emotions. It is a sign of emotional openness that is crucial in all healthy and meaningful relationships. It fosters a connection for deeper understanding and creates the empathy needed for long-term meaningful relationships.

You cannot expect others to understand you if you do not tell them what you need or want from them. This is impossible without vulnerability. Being too closed off can backfire. As mentioned in the previous section, you might be wearing different masks around different people. This not only creates a lot of internal chaos but makes the relationships less authentic too. It can make the bond unsatisfying. If this is the case, the chances of the relationship breaking are high. It also means the other person in the relationship will respond in ways deemed unsatisfactory. This is because you are not being honest. It can make you feel unsupported, build feelings of resentment, and blame them. In the end, you'll be left with shallow relationships.

It is okay if you're struggling to be vulnerable right now. It is okay if you cannot wear your heart on your sleeve. Regardless of what the reason is, you have the power to make yourself more vulnerable. Unless you open yourself to a relationship, it cannot be meaningful. Understand that you are your worst critic. The fear that others will judge you can be terrifying. This means we end up defending ourselves by hiding this fear. Ironically, the only way to overcome it is by making yourself vulnerable.

To open yourself, the first step is to discuss the vulnerability itself. Focus on sharing how you feel and discuss what it means with others. It is okay if you're struggling with it. In fact, this is perfectly normal. Whether it is childhood conditioning or life experiences, different things could have happened that prevent you from being vulnerable. When you share your struggles with others, it increases their ability to understand you. This means they learn to respond in more appropriate ways. It also makes it easier for them to support you the way you need it.

We all have a variety of fears. These fears get in the way of living the life we want. It prevents us from doing things we want because we are worried. Unfortunately, this fear will not go away unless you acknowledge and accept it. This probably sounds counterintuitive but it is incredibly effective. Your demons are scarier in your head than they actually are. When you confront them, the power or hold they have over you, reduces. In any relationship discussing your fears is a great way to bond. It makes you more human and strengthens the bond. It also lends an aspect of authenticity. Knowing that you are not alone in your fears by itself is comforting.

To be more vulnerable you need to live by your heart. It doesn't mean you have to always wear your heart on your sleeve. It is okay to be guarded but you should also know when you should let your guard down. How can you have a meaningful relationship when you're closed off by different walls? These walls might be in place to respect your boundaries or to prevent you from getting hurt. However, learn to focus on your heart. Go with what it wants. Even if you make mistakes, you can learn from them. The worst that will happen is if you will temporarily be disappointed. This is a small price to pay if it means you can be your authentic self.

Change is the only constant in life. Therefore, question your beliefs. Ask yourself what will happen if you open up? Even if your past was challenging, you can overcome it. You have a lot to gain and a little to lose by becoming vulnerable in a relationship.

Connecting With Others

Until now, you were introduced to different suggestions and tips that can be used to improve your communication skills. From making small talk to improving your body language, these things go a long way in forming healthy and meaningful relationships. Now, it is time to use those suggestions along with the ones given here to connect with others.

Be Approachable

You'll need to be approachable and friendly if you want to connect with others. If your words and actions convey that you appreciate someone, their willingness to reciprocate increases. This is known as reciprocal liking in psychology. It means you must be warm and friendly, offer genuine compliments, show that you are happy to meet someone and keep in touch. You will learn more about doing all this later. For now, remember that you cannot connect with someone unless you are friendly, to begin with.

The Common Ground

One point that was repeatedly stressed in the previous chapters is that you will need to find some common ground or shared interests. This is not only helpful for striking a conversation but bonding with them too. When you focus on some commonality instead of differences, it becomes easier to feel connected to others. It will also make them feel more connected to you. After all, birds of the same feather flock together. Whether it is love for a sport, movie series, or anything else, go ahead and find things you both like. When you have common interests, it becomes easier to bond. You can also schedule more meetings around these interests.

Be a Listener

You cannot connect with someone unless you are willing to listen to them. It's not just about hearing the words they say, instead you must become an active listener. The steps and suggestions to do this were introduced in the previous chapters. Good listening is needed for bonding. When you give someone your complete attention without giving in to any distractions, it shows them that they are a priority. It conveys a message that you value them. When a person feels valued, they will reciprocate. It sends a strong message that you care for them. This, in turn, will bring you closer.

Open Up

As mentioned earlier, if you want to strengthen your bond with anyone, you need to open up. Don't be an onion and don't wait for others to peel your layers. Don't keep your guard up at all times. There's something potent about bonding over shared insecurities, worries, and even fears. It not only makes you seem more relatable but shows that you care enough to share with them. It is okay if you don't want to get too personal right away. This is perfectly normal. When you focus on sharing a worry, insecurity, or fear, it builds trust. It means you are not scared to be a little vulnerable in front of the other person. This trust strengthens the conversations. For instance, you might be nervous about a big presentation at work. It is okay to share this nervousness with someone. They will not think less of you and you don't have to seem perfect. The more you share, the more human it makes you.

Spending Time Together

You cannot develop a stronger bond with anyone unless you start spending time together. Without this element, no relationship can fully evolve into something meaningful. Even in this digitized world we live in, the power of face-to-face conversations and time spent together cannot be underestimated.

In psychology, there is a term called the mere-exposure effect. It essentially refers to an increased liking or even a preference for a specific stimulus when an individual is repeatedly exposed to it. If we translate this to a real-life scenario, it means that spending time with someone regularly strengthens the bond you share with them. The chances of liking someone increase when they start becoming familiar with us. Even science supports this claim! If you want an acquaintance to become a good friend, you will need to spend around 140 hours together

((Jeffrey a. Hall, 2018). The same study also suggests that it takes around 300 hours to move from being a good friend to a best friend.

So, if you are interested in transforming a relationship with an acquaintance into something more meaningful, then you need to spend time together. Make plans to meet regularly. However, it doesn't mean you forget about all your other commitments and simply focus on spending time with one person. It is all about balance.

Receiving Feedback

Honesty is the cornerstone of any relationship. If you are pretending to be someone just to make others like you, it is a shallow relationship. It will always be superficial and will not manifest into anything deeper. To truly connect, be open to receiving feedback. It means you have to listen to certain topics or comments that are not easy for you. Real friends always tell the truth. Instead of defending, be open to accepting the feedback someone is giving you. Also, remember that whatever the other person is saying is their opinion and doesn't automatically become the truth. However, it gives you something to think about. Who knows, you might get a better understanding of yourself through all this?

Real Compliments

Sincere compliments show that you value the other person. It's not just about complimenting their clothes or something generic to gain their favor. Instead, it's about being genuine. If they stood by you through thick and thin, compliment them. We all love being complimented. These compliments are more powerful when they are genuine. When you receive praise, it creates a positive feeling. Ensure that your compliments are sincere and you're not saying things just for the sake of it.

Share Your Dreams and Goals

Another great way to deepen the connection with someone is to share your dreams, goals, and aspirations with them. There is vulnerability in putting forward your aspirations without any pretenses. Talking about your dreams is a wonderful bonding point. It is as potent as sharing your fears or insecurities. It takes a lot to talk about your dreams. Many shy away from doing this because they worry about how others might respond or what they would think. However, if you can let go of such doubts and worries and instead, put yourself out there, it will improve your relationship.

Face-To-Face Meetings

The world we live in is connected through the Internet. It is present in every aspect of our life and relationships are not an exception. Most relationships we have these days are through social media, messaging, and other forms of digital contact. However, these things do not and cannot replace the power of face-to-face meetings. If you want to deepen your bond with someone, prioritize meeting up over calling or texting them. These options may be efficient and are nice but being in the same room with someone makes it easier to understand who they are. It is also more intimate. Make a conscious effort to spend time together in the real world and not just in the digital space.

Favors Help

Asking for favors and doing favors increases trust. Do something spontaneous for the other person. Whether it is offering help with household chores or any work-related task, go ahead and do it. Even getting someone their favorite cup of coffee is good. These small favors show that you are listening to them and have paid attention to all that they have said. Don't do these favors to make the other person feel obligated to reciprocate. It's not about throwing the balance off in your relationship. Instead, it's about doing something without expecting anything in return.

Little acts of selflessness go a long way in strengthening the relationship.

If someone offers help or a favor, accept it. It doesn't make you smaller if you accept help from others. Accepting help and knowing when to ask for it, shows that you are aware of who you are. It also shows that you are not perfect. If you need some help, go ahead and ask. It will also make them feel better knowing that you count on them.

Be You

Well, it certainly sounds like there are a lot of things you need to do to build good relationships in life. Well, don't get too caught up in these rules and steps. You don't have to be perfect. You will learn along the way. A close relationship is always a direct validation of the person you are. It means it's an acceptance of who you are without any terms and conditions. So, ensure that you are your true self. If you are pretending to be someone, it is not a healthy relationship. If the other person makes you feel that you are supposed to pretend, it is certainly toxic. Be open and vulnerable. Let them into your life and don't be scared to enter theirs. If something feels amiss, then listen to your gut. You will learn more about this in the next chapter.

Caution to the Reader

Although I have mentioned that meaningful relationships add value to our life and should be pursued. It is important to also give caution. Not all relationships add value. From time to time you may run into people with toxic personality traits. These individuals can pull us into their world and make us feel less. It is important that you recognize these individuals and try not to pursue deep meaningful relationships with them. This is a topic that I take very seriously. Therefore, I have added a bonus chapter at the end of this book that addresses this issue.

Summary

Let's quickly summarize the key points that were discussed in this chapter:

- Communication is the key ingredient to building meaningful relationships.
- A meaningful relationship will provide the following benefits: better mental health, support, allows for growth, etc.
- In order to build meaningful relationships we have to be authentic and vulnerable.
- Utilize all of the communication guidance is this book to help pursue meaningful relationships.

Conclusion

Communication is the means to not just express yourself but also ensure your needs and requirements are met. Effective communication is needed in all aspects of life and isn't restricted to just professional relationships. Effective communication skills help smoothen your way with others and improve the quality of your relationships. However, struggling with this important skill is also quite common. Whether it is hesitance in approaching others, constant worrying while talking to strangers, or anxiety about making small talk, these are all obstacles that hinder your ability to effectively communicate. The good news is that you always have an option to change. If something is bothering you or you believe you are lagging in an aspect, with conscious effort, patience and consistency, you can change. You don't have to let poor communication skills get in the way of your life. You have complete control over changing this aspect about yourself.

It is never too late to change and this realization by itself can be quite empowering. You are the writer of your destiny. You needn't let the lack of proper communication skills hold you back. You have complete control over yourself and can change for the better. Remember, you don't have to implement all the changes at once. Instead, take things one day at a time and one step at a time. Focus on making and maintaining small changes given in this book. If you are willing to commit to this process and aren't scared of making some effort, you can reap all the benefits associated with becoming better at communicating. You don't have to hold yourself back. You can create the life you desire and achieve your personal and professional goals by becoming better at communicating. You don't have to dread interacting with others in any setting. It all starts with changing your mindset and attitude for the better. With a little patience, conscious effort, consistency, and self-awareness, you will become unstoppable.

Now that you have all the needed information and are equipped with the right tools, what are you waiting for? The next step is to go out there and implement the suggestions given in this book.

Bonus Chapter
Avoid Toxicity

Building meaningful relationships is important. This doesn't mean that everyone you come across is worthy of your time and attention. There will be those who bring you down or hold you back in one way or another. Whether it is a boss, family member, partner, friend, or even an acquaintance, toxic people are everywhere. The problem is that it is easy to identify some while others are tricky. Unless you are willing to live your life like a lone wolf, you will invariably cross paths with toxic individuals.

Anyone who causes any distress to someone through their words or actions is a toxic individual. The word toxic means different things to different individuals. A toxic label is usually placed on substances that cause harm such as chemicals and poisons. In terms of behavior, it refers to any unpleasant or malicious acts committed toward others.

A toxic individual is someone who is controlling, self-centered, manipulative in any form, and extremely needy. These individuals can be toxic due to their feelings of low self-esteem. It can also be caused by childhood trauma and other deeply seated personal issues. It can be a result of mental health problems such as narcissistic personality disorder. These individuals have dark core personality traits. It means they tend to put themselves, their goals and interests, and their needs over others. They will go to extreme lengths to cater to their needs and requirements. They do this by making others feel guilty or shameful to justify their malicious acts.

Identifying Toxic Individuals

To identify a toxic person, focus on yourself and how they make you feel. It's not just about what they say or do. Instead, notice how they make you feel and think about yourself. Here are some suggestions you can use to identify such individuals.

The individuals have no respect for boundaries. They will tirelessly go after what they want regardless of the consequences. It doesn't matter who gets hurt in the process. They will have no respect for your personal boundaries. Dealing with them will drain you out.

Toxic individuals are good at making you question your reality. Whether it is a manipulator or a narcissist, they are good at gaslighting. They create confusion that weakens their victims. If you are dealing with a toxic person, then chances are you are often confused about what is happening or has happened. If you come close to deciphering what they are doing, they will gaslight you. They will question your sanity and reality. This is because their words never align with their actions and vice versa. When you call them out on this dishonesty, they will call you unreasonable.

These individuals usually always play the role of the victim. They do this because they want to gain your sympathy. They want to make you feel that they have been wronged. They do this not just to deflect blame, but to justify their behavior. These individuals will never assume responsibility for being the problem. Instead, they will blame someone. To them, a relationship is a means to an end. They don't see anything wrong in not taking responsibility for their actions. They might blame it on you. They will also go out of their way to make all the wrongs seem right. If they acted inappropriately, they would have something to justify such behavior. They will also go to any length to blame their victims for their problems.

They will always be the center of conversations and situations. If they are not, they will do something to ensure the spotlight is on them. Even if you are talking about yourself, don't be surprised if the conversation somehow becomes about them. They will always try to one-up you. Regardless of what problem you have, a toxic individual will always have it worse. The message is that others should stop complaining because they are the center of the conversation. They will also consciously try to undermine any legitimacy of your complaints and remind you that they have graver problems in life.

Apart from all the suggestions mentioned here, trust your gut. If someone makes your internal alarm go off, listen to it. If your first impression of someone is they are up to no good or they are not good for you, go with it.

Why Avoid Them?

Now that you know how to recognize toxic individuals, learning why to avoid them is also needed. Even a toxic individual is a person but they are vicious. They are bad for your overall sense of well-being. Here are different reasons why avoiding them is needed.

Toxic individuals will make you always feel uncertain. Whether it is about yourself or life in general, they bring with them a sense of uncertainty. You never know what will make them tick. You never know how they will behave or what to expect. These things increase the stress you experience and leave you always feeling uncertain.

They also increase your self-doubt. When you are constantly plagued by self-doubt and confusion, you live a life filled with regret. This not only keeps you stuck in the past but prevents you from seeing all the good you have. It also harms your ability to create the future you want. Even when you take a step forward, this self-doubt increases confusion.

A combination of the factors mentioned until now increases your sense of anxiety. The constant doubt you are living in and their disregard increases anxiety. You start feeling anxious about the smallest things you say and do. When you overthink everything, living itself becomes challenging.

It makes you hyper vigilant. When you are dealing with a toxic individual, trusting others becomes challenging because you cannot even trust yourself. Once bitten twice shy is the norm you start living with because of all the manipulation you endured or are enduring.

You start losing interest in yourself and life. This is because of the emotional manipulation they subject you to. Life becomes mundane and you start treating every day with little or even no regard. You also start losing respect for yourself.

They also make you feel guilty and shameful. When you're constantly blamed for everything, it is difficult to not feel guilty. They will keep you trapped to ensure that you cater to their needs and requirements. Whether it is constant criticism or insecurity, shame becomes a constant companion.

It also increases self-isolation. Most toxic individuals maintain a stronghold on their victims. If you are a victim of a toxic person, they will try their best to keep you isolated. When all your strength and energy go to catering to their needs, you'll be left with nothing for yourself. This means you cannot focus on yourself or other healthy relationships. It, in turn, worsens the sense of isolation you feel.

When you are dealing with a toxic individual, your sense of self reduces. It also reduces your self-confidence. How can you trust yourself when you are constantly made to second guess and doubt everything you say and do? Understand that this is one of their manipulative techniques. Do not fall prey to it.

Toxic individuals are adept at telling others they are no good. When you are constantly told you are worthless or not good enough, you start looking for external approval. They use this to further intensify their hold on you.

It increases feelings of resentment, not just toward the toxic individual but yourself too. You can resent the person you have become. You can resent how they make you feel. All this creates a negative self-image.

Dealing With Toxic Individuals

An important thing you must remember while dealing with toxic individuals is that you are the only one responsible for yourself. You are not responsible for them regardless of what they portray. You also cannot change anybody and therefore, the best thing you can do is stop trying. Since you will invariably cross paths with toxic individuals at one point or another, learning to deal with them is the best thing you can do. This is needed for maintaining your sanity, inner peace, and happiness. In this section, let's look at some simple suggestions that can be easily implemented to deal with toxic individuals.

Self-Empowerment

Dealing with a toxic individual might make you feel as if you are powerless. You might know that you are not supposed to engage them or give in to them. However, not doing so means there will be consequences. Instead of feeling controlled, you'll need to make decisions from a position of power. Do not become a victim of their manipulation and instead, understand that you are responsible for yourself. If you don't want to do something, don't do it. Ensure that this decision comes from self-empowerment. If they want something from you, chances are you want something from them. Whether it is companionship, comfort in knowing that you have a relationship, or anything else along these lines, decide if it is worth it. If all these things are sabotaging your life, what is the point of holding on to the relationship? With a little self-awareness, it becomes easier to make helpful decisions.

Understand What They See in You

A toxic individual always sees in others what they don't want to see in themselves. Everything that they don't acknowledge or accept about themselves they see in you. This is known as projection. Even if you are generous, empathetic, and hardworking, they will see you as a liar, slacker, manipulator, and someone toxic. Understand that what they are saying about you is a reflection of themselves. They are not talking about you and instead, are talking about themselves. When you know and can differentiate this from yourself, it becomes easier to maintain your distance from them.

Set and Implement Boundaries

You cannot make everyone happy and you cannot please everyone. Once you understand this truth, it becomes easier to deal with a toxic individual. They can make you believe that you are responsible for them and this will make you work harder and compromise more. All this is ultimately exhausting and draining. These individuals are good at tearing down your boundaries and walking all over you before you even realize what has happened. The simplest way to overcome this is by drawing your boundaries and implementing them. If you believe something is unacceptable, put your foot down. Don't feel guilty about it and do not let anyone encroach your boundaries. It is not worth it. It doesn't matter what others think. As long as you are living your life based on your values, dealing with them becomes easier.

You Are Not Responsible for Them

It might seem as if a toxic individual is always in a crisis of one form or another. Even if they are not, they are good at creating them. They thrive when there is drama. In such instances, understand that they are creating this crisis to gain your sympathy, empathy, and support. You don't have to run to their aid. You don't have to be a part of their pity party. You are not responsible for them. As mentioned, you are responsible only for yourself. Similarly, they are responsible for everything that happens to them. You might feel bad, but remember that you are not dealing with a normal person. They are toxic for a reason, and you are not responsible for them regardless of what they say or do.

No Explanations

Saying "no" probably sounds simpler than it is. Most people struggle to say no. The most common reason is the fear of rejection and judgment. Understand that "no" by itself is a complete sentence. It is one of the most powerful words in any language. If you say no to someone or something, it is a complete answer. You don't owe them any explanations whatsoever. As long as you know what you want and don't, saying no becomes easier. Once you implement your boundaries, saying no also becomes easier.

You do not need their approval. Period. This is one truth you must accept. Stop looking for external sources of approval. You are sufficient how you are. All the approval you need must come from within. Understand that their approval and acceptance always come with terms and conditions. As mentioned, a healthy and meaningful relationship offers this without any strings attached. If someone likes you only when you do things their way, it is not healthy.

Do Not Judge

You should be kind, respectful, compassionate, and understanding. However, you must first direct this toward yourself. You don't have to turn yourself into someone you don't want to be. If someone is doing this to you, they are toxic. Strength and compassion can coexist even when you have boundaries in place. Instead of judging them, focus on yourself. Judging them is a waste of your mental and emotional strength and energy. It is not good for your health. Judging them will also give you nothing in return. Instead, focus on your boundaries. You'll feel better.

Understand Yourself

Just because someone says you are bad at something; it doesn't make it true. Unless you act on and accept what others say, it cannot become your reality. For instance, if someone says you are a slacker, it doesn't automatically make you one. So, it is time for self-introspection. You must understand yourself. This means you must not only accept your strengths but acknowledge your weaknesses too. When you know yourself inside out, no one can convince you otherwise. This self-awareness automatically takes away their power over you. They may attempt to send verbal comments to demoralize you, but you can rest easy in knowing who you are. When you are aware of your weaknesses, no one can overpower you by using them against you. What they think will not matter. This is liberating by itself. It also means you can focus on creating the life you want.

Stop Expecting Change

Previously, it was mentioned that you must not expect change from a toxic individual. Regardless of how heartfelt their promises are, they will not change. This is one of the reasons why they are toxic. Once you know where you stand, don't waver. You don't need anything more than this. Even if they try to bend or break you, walk away. Doing this becomes easier once you understand and accept how you are. Always remember that they are not motivated by what is good for you or the relationship. It will always be about them. Whatever they say and do is to serve their needs and purposes. If you keep expecting them to change, you are opening yourself up for manipulation and more heartbreak. You will continue the cycle of toxicity if you do not stand your ground.

Choose Your Battles

Dealing with a toxic individual is draining. Whether it is your personal or professional life, they are energy-sucking vampires. Therefore, you will need to choose your battles wisely. They will try to trigger you and create drama. It is entirely up to you whether you give in to this or not. Do not become their victim and do not sustain that toxicity. As much as possible, try to avoid them. Whether it is in the physical world or the digital realm, maintain your distance from them. You do not need them in your life.

No Victimization

When you are dealing with a toxic individual, the chances of indulging in self-pity increases. You can feel sorry and bad for yourself. You probably feel bad that you passed on many opportunities because of them. You probably feel bad that you did not accept yourself and take control of your life because of them. Instead of victimizing yourself, understand that you have boundaries. You are strong, smart, and capable enough to make decisions that are good for you. You can thrive. When you know that you are the one in charge of your life, it is quite freeing. Victimization will simply drain your energy and make you feel bad. Living your life in the past or with regrets is going to cloud your future. Instead, focus on a future you want to create.

Focus on Solution

A toxic individual in any aspect of your life can make you bend over backward to ensure that you are there for them. This will make you feel disempowered and believe that you have no control over yourself or life in general. It also increases resentment. Understand that you do not have to solve their problems for them. It is not your mess to clean up. They are the only ones to blame. Do not focus on their negative behavior instead, try to see what you can do to make yourself feel better. Focus on solving the problem and getting out of the relationship.

The solution might not always be easy. Usually, the best thing you can do is break your ties with them and move away. Moving away emotionally, mentally, and physically from them is good for your health and well-being. Forgive them for whatever they have put you through. Forgiveness is empowering and relieving. It enables you to focus on the future instead of living in the past. Remember that you do not have to forget to forgive them. You can forgive and move on. Learn your lessons and cut your losses. It is okay as long as you know what you should not be doing in the future. Whatever has happened cannot be changed. There is no point in blaming them or yourself. Forgive and move on.

Build Healthy Relationships

Use all the suggestions given in this book to develop healthier and more meaningful relationships. Focus on channeling your energy into something better. Stop dwelling on the past and surround yourself with those who mean well to you. When you surround yourself with positive people and those who wish the best for you, you will feel better. It also increases your internal strength to stand by your decisions. You have the power to choose and choose wisely.

Thank You

I just want to say thank you for reading my book.

There are several other books that you could have picked from, but you chose this one, and it means so much to me.

So, THANK YOU, for getting this book and for reading it all the way to the very end.

Before you go, I have a small favor to ask. **If you enjoyed reading this book and found the information helpful, can you spare a couple of minutes and leave a review on Amazon? Posting a review is the best way to support the work of authors like me.**

Your feedback is important and I would love to keep writing books that will help you obtain the results you are seeking for.

Thank you and all the best!

To leave a review, you can use the QR Codes below to redirect you to the Amazon website

Amazon US:

Amazon UK:

Amazon CA:

References

Active Listening vs Passive Listening: Is One Better Than the Other? (2020, July 30). Lifehack. https://www.lifehack.org/881336/passive-listening

Ambady, N., & Rosenthal, R. (1993). Half a minute: Predicting teacher evaluations from thin slices of nonverbal behavior and physical attractiveness. *Journal of Personality and Social Psychology, 64*(3), 431–441. https://doi.org/10.1037/0022-3514.64.3.431

Bowe, J. (2021, August 17). *People who are good at small talk always avoid these 7 mistakes, says public speaking expert.* CNBC. https://www.cnbc.com/2021/08/17/avoid-these-mistakes-if-you-want-to-be-good-at-small-talk-says-public-speaking-expert.html

Changing Habits - Learning Center. (2019). Learning Center. https://learningcenter.unc.edu/tips-and-tools/changing-habits/

Childs, C. (2007, July 4). *How To Start a Conversation with Anyone.* Lifehack. https://www.lifehack.org/articles/communication/how-to-initiate-conversation.html

Delony, J. (2022, April 13). *How to Start a Conversation With a Real-Life Human Being.* Ramsey Solutions. https://www.ramseysolutions.com/relationships/how-to-start-a-conversation

DiNuzzo, E. (2021, August 3). *12 Rude Conversation Habits You Need to Stop ASAP*. Reader's Digest. https://www.rd.com/list/rude-conversation-habits/

Duhigg, C. (2012, March 5). *Habits: How They Form And How To Break Them*. NPR.org. https://www.npr.org/2012/03/05/147192599/habits-how-they-form-and-how-to-break-them#:~:text=Neuroscientists%20have%20traced%20our%20habit

Ethans, L. (2021, March 18). *6 Health Benefits Of Deeper Relationships*. Power of Positivity: Positive Thinking & Attitude. https://www.powerofpositivity.com/6-health-benefits-of-deeper-relationships/

Five Benefits of Tracking your Mood. (2022, April 30). Calm Blog. https://blog.calm.com/blog/5-benefits-of-tracking-your-mood

Gilbert, R. (n.d.). *Why Body Language Matters Speak To Your Patients Without Saying a Word*. https://wmc.wa.gov/sites/default/files/public/9.%20Why%20Body%20Language%20Matters%20-%20Renee%20Gilbert-%20Ph.D..pdf

Gould, W. R. (2021, September 20). *Why Vulnerability in Relationships Is So Important*. Verywell Mind. https://www.verywellmind.com/why-vulnerability-in-relationships-is-so-important-5193728

Hall, J. A. (2018). How many hours does it take to make a friend? *Journal of Social and Personal*

Relationships, 36(4), 1278–1296. https://doi.org/10.1177/0265407518761225

Hurd, S. (2021, July 9). *6 Annoying Conversational Habits That Push People Away - Learning Mind*. Www.learning-Mind.com. https://www.learning-mind.com/annoying-conversational-habits/

Ho, L. (2020, November 6). *The Psychology of Habit Formation (And How to Hack it)*. Lifehack. https://www.lifehack.org/889303/habit-formation

How Much of Communication Is Nonverbal? | UT Permian Basin Online. (2020, November 3). Online.utpb.edu. https://online.utpb.edu/about-us/articles/communication/how-much-of-communication-is-nonverbal/

Lancia, G. (n.d.). *Starting a Conversation -The ARE Method*. https://positivepsychology.com/wp-content/uploads/2021/05/Starting-a-Conversation-The-ARE-Method.pdf

Logie, J. (2020). *3 Ways a Negative Mindset Is Ruining Your Life & How to Beat It - Learning Mind*. Www.learning-Mind.com. https://www.learning-mind.com/negative-mindset-beat/

MacLeod, C. (2020). *Some Common Conversation Mistakes | www.succeedsocially.com*. Succeedsocially.com. https://www.succeedsocially.com/conversationmistakes

Master the Art of Small Talk in 7 Steps. (2020, May 2). Inc.com. https://www.inc.com/youngentreprenuer-council/master-art-of-small-talk-in-7-steps.html

McCallum, K. (2021, January 18). *Habits: How We Make Them & How We Can Break Them*. Www.houstonmethodist.org. https://www.houstonmethodist.org/blog/articles/2 021/jan/habits-how-we-make-them-and-how-we-can-break-them/

Morin, D. A. (2020, January 23). *23 Tips to Bond With Someone (And Form a Deep Connection)*. SocialPro. https://socialself.com/blog/how-to-bond/

Morin, D., & Wendler, D. (2021, August 25). *How to Start a Conversation (Without Being Awkward)*. SocialPro. https://socialself.com/start-conversation/

Reddy, C. (2016, April 26). *Small Talk - Importance, Benefits, Purpose and Tips - WiseStep*. https://content.wisestep.com/small-talk-importance-benefits-purpose/

Reichard, G. (n.d.). *Authenticity - The Power of Being Authentic*. https://www.coachingbreakthroughs.ca/authenticit y/the-power-of-being-authentic/

Saraev, N. (2020, August 27). *Nine Bad Body Language Habits You Need To Stop, Yesterday*. Medium. https://nicksaraev.medium.com/nine-bad-body-language-habits-you-need-to-stop-yesterday-92dd5549e71a

Scott, E. (2018). *How to Reduce Negative Self-Talk for a Better Life*. Verywell Mind. https://www.verywellmind.com/negative-self-talk-and-how-it-affects-us-4161304

Tanzeem, S. (2021, December 6). *What Is a Mood Tracker? How to Use It Effectively*. MUO. https://www.makeuseof.com/mood-tracker-how-to-use/

Ten Expert Tips on How to Overcome Social Anxiety. (2021, October 31). Nick Wignall. https://nickwignall.com/social-anxiety/

The Best Ways to Start a Conversation With a Stranger. (2021, June 9). Home of Influence. https://homeofinfluence.com/the-best-ways-to-start-a-conversation-with-a-stranger/

The Role Of Body Language In Communication. (2020, September 3). Harappa. https://harappa.education/harappa-diaries/how-to-improve-body-language/

Tung, J., & Milbr, L. (2021). *10 Tips for Making Small Talk Less Awkward*. Real Simple. https://www.realsimple.com/work-life/work-life-etiquette/manners/10-big-rules-small-talk

Waters, S. (2021, September 20). *How to read body language and gain deeper emotional awareness*. Www.betterup.com. https://www.betterup.com/blog/how-to-read-body-language

Young, K. (2015, July 6). *Toxic People: 16 Practical, Powerful Ways to Deal With Them*. Hey Sigmund. https://www.heysigmund.com/toxic-people-16-practical-powerful-ways-to-deal-with-them/

Young, K. (2015, April 10). *Vulnerability: The Key to Close Relationships* -. Heysigmund.com. https://www.heysigmund.com/vulnerability-the-key-to-close-relationships/

Zetlin, M. (2015, May 27). *11 Foolproof Ways to Start a Conversation With Absolutely Anyone*. Inc.com. https://www.inc.com/minda-zetlin/10-foolproof-ways-to-start-a-conversation-with-absolutely-anyone.html

Made in the USA
Columbia, SC
14 September 2024

42244573R00088